Praise for *The Nature M...*

'With innumerable gems and n...
curiosity, *The Nature Magpie* is a repository of ...
treasures.'
Chris Packham

'Not so much trivia titbits as intellectual petits fours ... a daily
dip will be sure to prompt discussion, wonder and compulsive
retelling.'
BBC Wildlife Magazine

'Difficult to resist. For anyone interested in the natural world
there are myriad facts and figures that will fascinate and
surprise.'
Alexandra Henton, *The Field*

'Allen's book promises a cornucopia of facts ... It delivers just
that, providing a bran tub full of informational morsels.'
Fortean Times

'A miscellany that keeps you turning the pages.'
Desmond Morris, author of *The Naked Ape*

'*The Nature Magpie* is seductively readable, a delightful and
constantly surprising compendium of facts about nature.'
Bill Adams, author of *Against Extinction: The Story of Conservation*

'A delightful lucky dip of fascinating facts.'
Kate Long, author of *The Bad Mother's Handbook*

The
Nature Magpie

**A cornucopia of facts, anecdotes,
folklore and literature from
the natural world**

DANIEL ALLEN

ICON

First published in the UK in 2013 by
Icon Books Ltd, Omnibus Business Centre,
39–41 North Road, London N7 9DP
email: info@iconbooks.net
www.iconbooks.net

This edition published in the UK in 2014 by Icon Books Ltd

Sold in the UK, Europe and Asia
by Faber & Faber Ltd, Bloomsbury House,
74–77 Great Russell Street,
London WC1B 3DA or their agents

Distributed in the UK, Europe and Asia
by TBS Ltd, TBS Distribution Centre, Colchester Road,
Frating Green, Colchester CO7 7DW

Distributed in Australia and New Zealand
by Allen & Unwin Pty Ltd,
PO Box 8500, 83 Alexander Street,
Crows Nest, NSW 2065

Distributed in South Africa by Jonathan Ball,
Office B4, The District, 41 Sir Lowry Road,
Woodstock 7925

Distributed in the USA by
Consortium Book Sales & Distribution,
The Keg House, 34 Thirteenth Avenue NE, Suite 101,
Minneapolis, MN 55413-1007

Distributed in Canada by Penguin Books Canada,
90 Eglinton Avenue East, Suite 700,
Toronto, Ontario M4P 2YE

ISBN: 978-184831-658-4

Typeset in ITC Stone by Marie Doherty

Printed and bound in the UK
by Clays Ltd, St Ives plc

Dedicated to my parents,
Janice and Tim Allen

In memory of Neville Allen (1930–2005)
My Nature Magpie

ABOUT THE AUTHOR

Daniel Allen is a writer, editor, otter expert, independent scholar and fellow of the Royal Geographical Society. He writes for a number of publications, including regular columns in *Small Furry Pets* and *Practical Reptile Keeping* magazines. Daniel's first book, *Otter*, was published in 2010. Virginia McKenna OBE described it as 'the most brilliant mix of facts ancient and modern about the otter species'.

Daniel comes from an academic background, having gained a PhD in Human Geography from the University of Nottingham in 2006 before going on to lecture at Keele University.

More information about Daniel's expertise and availability can be found on his personal website:

www.drdanielallen.co.uk

CONTENTS

'Nature is a book of many pages and each page
tells a fascinating story'
—Andrew Ellicott Douglas (1867–1962)

'What a book a devil's chaplain might write on
the clumsy, wasteful, blundering, low, and horribly
cruel work of nature.'
—Charles Darwin (1809–1882)

INTRODUCTION

'It seems to me that the natural world is the
    greatest source of excitement;
the greatest source of visual beauty; the greatest
    source of intellectual interest.
It is the greatest source of so much in life that
    makes life worth living.'
                                    —Sir David Attenborough

Nature is one of the most widely talked about subjects in the 21st century. Every day, reports about natural disasters, the weather, calls to save endangered species, animal mistreatment, and the threat of virus and disease abound in the news. In these debates, ideas about nature are often multiple and contradictory, but everyone is united in sharing personal experiences with the natural world.

Our past influences our attitudes towards nature – whether it was the first time you looked into the eyes of a captive animal in a zoo, family holidays to exotic places, sleeping beneath the stars in a national park, watching wildlife documentaries, learning how to identify birds and forage with your grandfather or walking in the rain with a girlfriend or boyfriend, everybody has had their special moments with nature.

In childhood, watching *Tarka the Otter* as a six-year-old very much influenced my approach to the natural world. Expecting a Disney-inspired cartoon with talking animals, a love story and a happy ending, I was met with barking dogs, hunting horns, blood, death and misery. This traumatic experience may have inspired some to become hunt saboteurs in later life – it had a different effect on me. Not only did it ignite my obsession with otters, it influenced my curiosity for the natural world, and started a lifelong inclination of questioning absolutely everything, while respecting the responses, however unsavoury.

I, as your candid corvid guide, am an animal geographer, otter expert, conservationist, pet magazine columnist and animal welfarist. The enormity of nature can be daunting, yet the briefest of moments inspires joy and fear. *The Nature Magpie* plays on these emotions, picking the choicest morsels from history, literature, philosophy, science and more to bring you a unique, fragmentary but many-sided look at the natural world. I hope you enjoy it.

IN THE BEGINNING

'In the beginning God created the heavens and the earth' are the first words of the Book of Genesis. The Judeo-Christian story of creation is a prominent world-view. Literal interpretations date the earth as 6,000–10,000 years old, and creationists believe every aspect of the natural world was created in six days:

Day 1: God created light and separated the light from the darkness, calling light 'day' and darkness 'night'.

Day 2: God created an expanse to separate the waters and called it 'sky'.

Day 3: God created the dry ground and gathered the waters, calling the dry ground 'land' and the gathered waters 'seas'. On day three, God also created vegetation.

Day 4: God created the sun, moon, and stars to give light to the earth and to govern and separate the day and the night. These would also serve as signs to mark seasons, days, and years.

Day 5: God created every living creature of the seas and every winged bird, blessing them to multiply and fill the waters and the sky with life.

Day 6: God created animals to fill the earth. On day six, God also created man and woman in his own image to commune with him. He blessed them and gave them every creature and the whole earth to rule over, care for, and cultivate.

Day 7: God had finished his work of creation and so he rested on the seventh day, blessing it and making it holy.

This is just one of many creation myths. Thousands of years ago, humans tried to make sense of the origins of the natural world in which they exist and the ethnic culture within which they are grouped. Here are a few other examples of these sacred symbolic narratives:

Daoist

'The Way gave birth to unity, Unity gave birth to duality, Duality gave birth to trinity, Trinity gave birth to the myriad creatures. The myriad creatures bear yin on their back and embrace yang in their bosoms. They neutralise these vapours and thereby achieve harmony.'

—Daodejing, 4th century BC

Midewin

Great Rabbit, the servant of the God Spirit, saw the helpless condition of the original people. He wanted them to overcome starvation and disease. After choosing an otter to communicate with the people, he shared the secrets of the Midewin, handing the animal the sacred drum, rattle, and tobacco for curing the sick. Using his medicine bag he then 'shot' a sacred white shell, the mi'gis, into the body of the otter, giving him immortality and the ability to pass on these secrets. The widespread use of otter-skin medicine bags in healing ceremonies was influenced by this myth.

Ojibwe

'Kitche Manitou, the Great Spirit, had a vision, a dream. He made the earth, the rocks, water, fire and wind. He made the plants, animals, fishes, birds, and insects and then the Original People, Anishinabe, last ...

Kitche Manitou then made The Great Laws of nature so that all living things could live in harmony and balance. The Great Laws governed the place and movement of the sun, moon, earth and stars; the powers of wind, water, fire and rock; the rhythm and continuity of life, birth, growth and decay. All things lived and worked by these laws.'

—Native Drums website (http://www.native-drums.ca)

Zulu

'Unkulunkulu, the Ancient One, is the Zulu creator. He originally broke off from the reeds ... It was he who broke off the people from the reeds and then the cattle and other peoples. He also broke off medicine men and dreams. He was really the first man and progenitor of other men. He created everything that is – mountains, cattle, stream, snakes. He taught the Zulu how to hunt, how to make fire with sticks, and how to eat corn. He named the animals for them.'

—David Adams Leeming, *Creation Myths of the World: An Encyclopedia* (2010)

> 'Anyone teaching Historical Geology is faced with students who have already concluded that creationism explains the history of the earth. One of the questions that perplexes me is how such students can conclude that their ethnic or religious group has the complete explanation of the origin of the earth and its life, when so many ethnic or religious groups have so many different accounts of those origins.'
> —Bruce Railsback, geologist at the University of Georgia

SPECIES DISCOVERIES

Every year over 19,000 species are discovered and officially named. As you might imagine, this is quite a challenge for the taxonomists involved. In 2008 the International Institute for Species Exploration (IISE) was set up to help advance the taxonomic process. The public have also been encouraged to take part, by nominating the 'most exciting and engaging' finds. These then appear on an annual Top Ten New Species list. Here is the 2012 list of species described in 2011:

1. A snub-nosed monkey from Myanmar, Burma, that sneezes when it rains
   Name: Sneezing Monkey (*Rhinopithecus strykeri*)

2. A brightly coloured venomous banded box jellyfish, presumed to make those who first encounter it exclaim 'Oh boy!'
   Name: Bonaire Banded Box Jellyfish (*Tamoya ohboya*)

3. A nematode measuring just half a millimetre found at a depth of 1.3km (0.8 mile) in a South African gold mine.
Name: Devil's Worm (*Halicephalobus mephisto*)

4. The first night-blooming orchid. It grows in the tropical forests of Papua New Guinea.
Name: Night-blooming Orchid (*Bulbophyllum nocturnum*)

5. A small parasitic wasp that attacks and deposits eggs into unsuspecting desert ants in less than 0.05 seconds.
Name: Small Attack Wasp (*Kollasmosoma sentum*)

6. A sponge-like mushroom which resembles a popular cartoon character.
Name: Spongebob Squarepants Mushroom (*Spongiforma squarepantsii*)

7. A yellow poppy that blooms in the autumn monsoon season. Found hidden away miles into the Himalayan wilderness.
Name: Nepalese Autumn Poppy (*Meconopsis autumnalis*)

8. A millipede found in Tanzania's Eastern Arc Mountains, which is so big it looks like a sausage.
Name: Wandering Leg Sausage (*Crurifarcimen vagans*)

9. A fossil of an extinct creature that may have used its bristly legs to capture prey.
Name: Walking Cactus (*Diania cactiformis*)

10. An iridescent blue tarantula found in Brazil's Amazon basin.

Name: Sazima's Tarantula (*Pterinopelma sazimai*)

PANDA DIPLOMACY

Known for delivering information with a gentle authority, British naturalist Chris Packham is 'excited by everything that slithers, slimes, scratches and stings'. Much to the surprise of the public, the giant panda did not fall into this category. In 2009 he stated:

> Here is a species that, of its own accord, has gone down an evolutionary cul-de-sac ...Unfortunately, it's big and cute and a symbol of the World Wide Fund for Nature and we pour millions of pounds into panda conservation ... I reckon we should pull the plug. Let them go, with a degree of dignity.

Although he later apologised, these comments did raise debate, which Packham insists was always the intention. His point, however undiplomatic, also remains valid. There are just 1,600 pandas in the wild and 328 in captivity. Over the past 30 years the Chinese authorities have reintroduced just ten captive-bred pandas to the wild. One died, another was killed by wild pandas, and six lost so much weight they were sent back to the Chengdu Giant Panda Field Research Centre.

Pandas have become more than an endangered species. Their presence puts a zoo on the global conservation map, bringing worldwide publicity. As Henry Nicholls, author of *The Way of The Panda* (2010), explains: 'The real value of captive pandas lies not in their identity as pandas but in the colossal symbolic importance we humans have invested in this remarkable species.' Giving up on the panda would save money, but admitting defeat on the most high-profile endangered species would be far more costly for global conservation.

> 'Well-run zoos are an aid to animals and are not detrimental to their well-being ... indeed, in many cases, zoos will turn out to be the last refuge of numerous species in a human-being-infested world.'
>
> Gerald Durrell, *The Stationary Ark,* 1976

SHIPS OF THE DESERT

Ungainly, uncomfortable, bad-tempered, smelly creatures with a propensity to spit is how most holiday makers remember their encounters with camels. When Jacqueline Kennedy, the US First Lady, visited Pakistan in 1962 she reluctantly had a ride, sitting on a heavily gilded two-seat howdah. 'A camel makes an elephant feel like a jet plane,' Kennedy later remarked.

Of the two species of camel, it was the two-humped bactrian (*Camelus bactrianus*) from central Asia that Kennedy rode. The one-humped dromedary (*Camelus dromedaries*) is native to the Middle East and Africa. Alongside geographic location, another useful way of distinguishing which has one hump or two is in the first letter of the respective names: B has two humps, D has one.

Most of the world's 14 million camels are domesticated. Of these, 90 per cent are Dromedaries. Historically, these desert dwellers have been highly valued as transportable wealth, much like the horse and cow in more temperate environments. Their roles, as *Fifty Animals that Changed the Course of History* author Eric Chaline points out, include 'beasts of burden, war mounts, milk producers and meat animals'. Without them, surviving the extreme desert conditions would be impossible.

These camels have adapted perfectly to the dry, hot, cold, sandy conditions of desert life. The hump is a prime asset. Contrary to popular belief, this is not full of water. It is a mound of fat internally consumed as an emergency food supply. Dromedaries can drink 113.5 litres (30 gallons) of water in ten minutes, and prevent sweating by varying their body temperature from 34 to 41.7°C. Their bodies are water-saving units that can go without water for up to seven days in the hottest of temperatures. Even their urine is highly concentrated and their dung dry.

As well as being able to carry four times the weight (up to 650lbs/295kg) of most packhorses, these ungulates have wide, tough, leathery feet designed not to sink. Moving both legs on the same side of the body together makes them more stable on the sand. During sandstorms their vision is also protected by thick, long eyelashes. These qualities made this animal vital to cross-desert trade over the centuries, connecting the Middle East with North Africa and Europe.

Camels may not be the most comfortable of rides, or the friendliest of animals, but they did help shape the history of the world, allowing international trade to cross continents, making nations powerful and merchants rich.

Camels are even-toed ungulates (*Artiodactyla*) – hoofed animals whose weight is spread equally on the third and fourth toes ('ungulates' are simply mammals with hoofs). Other animals in this group include the antelope, cow, deer, goat, giraffes, hippopotamus, sheep and pig. Odd-toed ungulates (*Perissodactyla*), which have one or three toes, include the horse, rhinoceroses and zebra. The Smithsonian Institution recognises 257 modern ungulates. A hoof is a modified toenail.

HOPPING AROUND

If you happen to be in Tasmania and see wallabies hopping in circles around fields with a little more bounce than normal, it's OK, trust your eyes. It's highly unlikely you are hallucinating. The wallabies, on the other hand, may well be. As the world's largest producer of legally grown opium, Tasmania has an unlikely mob of drug-fuelled marsupials. In June 2009 the then Attorney General of the State, Lara Giddings, announced, 'We have a problem with wallabies entering poppy fields, getting as high as a kite and going around in circles.

Then they crash.' Giddings continued, 'We see crop circles in the poppy industry from wallabies that are high.'

Across the world the media had fun with the story. Happy hops damaging poppy crops, high wallabies making crop circles, more trippy than Skippy, opiate-crazed pouchers. The bizarre behaviour was not a laughing matter for everyone. During the previous financial year, a total of 2,280 poppy heads were stolen. Deer and sheep had also been known to snack on the nutritious narcotics. The field operations manager of Tasmanian Alkaloids, Rick Rockliff, told *The Mercury*:

> As growers we try our best to try and stop this sort of consumption, particularly by livestock, due to concerns about the contamination of the meat. There is also the risk to our poppy stocks, so growers take this very seriously but there has been a steady increase in the number of wild animals and that is where we are having difficulty keeping them off our land.

These concerns are understandable. The land of the two Tasmanian pharmaceutical companies licensed to take medicinal products from poppies covers an enormous 49,420 acres. That's an awful lot of wallaby-proof fencing. So how do you stop wallabies from hopping into your land? A 2010 report by the Tasmanian Institute for Agricultural Research gave the following advice: 'Wallaby-proof fencing is a long-term option that usually needs to be integrated with other control methods such as shooting, poisoning and trapping, both at establishment and over time.'

MAKING TRACKS

Identifying birds by song can take years to master; identifying mammals by tracks is much easier. You just need a bit of guidance and plenty of practice.

Red foxes (*Vulpes vulpes*) do not keep to regular trails. Their four-digit tracks are very similar to those of dogs, but far more compact. The outer toes curve towards the inner ones. There is also space for a horizontal line to separate the upper and lower toes.

Fore   *Hind*

Badgers (*Meles meles*) generally keep to well-worn trails within the territory around their sett. Look for five-digit prints with a large kidney-shaped pad. The digits almost appear in a line, the fifth not always registering. In soft mud the claw prints also show. Another clue nearby can be their coarse white-tipped hair, which often gets caught on the bark of trees and barbed wire fencing.

Fore   *Hind*

Otters (*Lutra lutra*) are always on the move. Any warm, empty shelter close to the water can become their holt for the day. They leave behind five-toed impressions with a rounded pad. Sometimes the webbing can be seen. Spraints (otter droppings) are also strategically deposited to mark their territory.

Fore   Hind

Mink (*Neovison vison*) tracks are sometimes mistaken for those of otters. Mink do leave behind five-toed impressions but they are smaller in size and have a star-shaped appearance. Imprints of long sharp claws are often visible, as is slight webbing. The heel pad, or interdigital, has four lobes, the largest two in the middle. **Weasel** (*Mustela nivalis*) prints are similar but much smaller.

Mink:

Fore   Hind

Weasel:

Fore   Hind

Water voles (*Arvicola terrestris*) live in waterside burrows. Each forefoot has four digital pads with distinct claws, giving the impression of the toes being pointed. Each hind foot has five digital pads, with similar claws. A well-formed print looks like a miniature human hand.

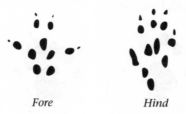

Fore   *Hind*

Brown rat (*Rattus norvegicus*) tracks are similar to those of water voles in shape and size, although the hind foot leaves a longer and narrower heel pattern. **Wood mouse** (*Apodemus sylvaticus*) tracks also resemble this but on a smaller scale.

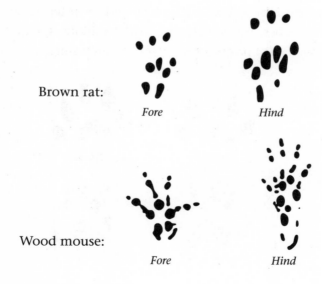

Brown rat:

Fore   *Hind*

Wood mouse:

Fore   *Hind*

Grey squirrels (*Sciurus carolinensis*) have similar size prints to rats but can leave a complicated series of pad and claw marks. Those of **red squirrels** (*Sciurus vulgaris*) are smaller. The jumping movement of squirrels also groups their tracks, with hind prints appearing ahead of front ones.

Fore   *Hind*

Hedgehogs (*Erinaceus europaeus*) leave quite different tracks from the fore and hind feet, which can be confusing. The forefeet have five toes, but the thumb-like digit is often faint. The hind feet are narrower and longer with three toes in a row and two set further back. There are also three fused interdigital pads, and two heel pads on all feet.

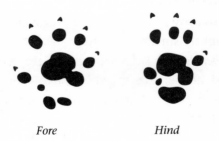

Fore   *Hind*

Rabbits (*Oryctolagus cuniculus*) are easy to identify, with four digits on each foot and no heel pads. Their hind legs also leave long exaggerated impressions.

Fore   Hind

WHAT IS THE DIFFERENCE BETWEEN A ...?

Similarities in appearance between certain species mean that mistaken identity is a common occurrence. Here are some tips to help see the differences.

House sparrow and tree sparrow:

House sparrows (*Passer domesticus*) have black and brown feathers, light grey breast and cheeks, a short, thick beak and grey crown. Females are much lighter in colour.

Tree sparrows (*Passer montanus*) have all chestnut brown crowns, white cheeks and collar and a contrasting black cheek spot.

House sparrows are noisy and gregarious. Tree sparrows are slightly smaller and shyer.

Remember: House sparrows have a grey crown like a slate roofed house; tree sparrows have a brown crown like trees in the winter; hedge sparrows are not sparrows at all, look for their slender, sharp beaks.

Song thrush and mistle thrush

Song thrushes (*Turdus philomelos*) have rich brown arrow-shaped marks on their cream under-body.

Mistle thrushes (*Turdus viscivorus*) have rounded blotches on their under-body, with distinctive white tail edges.

Black carrion crow and rook

Black carrion crows (*Corvus corone*) have feathers covering their face and the top of their thick beak.

Rooks (*Corvus frugilegus*) have bare faces, revealing a grey-white skin at the base of the beak.

Black carrion crows nest as one pair, and are fairly solitary.

Rooks nest in colonies (rookery), and are usually seen in flocks. They are often seen together with jackdaws (*Corvus monedula*) – distinctive by their grey nape and silvery white eyes.

Remember: As the old saying goes, 'If there's more than one crow they are rooks, if there is only one rook it's a crow.'

Grey wolf and coyote

Grey wolves (*Canis lupus*) have a large blocky face and muzzle, and shorter rounded ears.

Coyotes (*Canis latrans*) have a narrow pointed face and muzzle, and taller pointed ears.

Grey wolves are larger, approximately 2ft 6ins (76cm) tall at the shoulder and 6ft (1.8m) in length. They also hunt in packs.

Coyotes are generally shorter and smaller. They primarily hunt alone or in pairs.

Remember: Wolf pups in midsummer closely resemble coyotes.

Grizzly bear and black bear

Grizzly bears (*Ursus arctos horribilis*) have relatively long hair, usually with grizzled lighter tips, and a distinct shoulder hump.

Black bears (*Ursus americanus*) often have a lighter patch on their chest, and lack a shoulder hump.

Grizzly bears have a depression between the eyes and the end of the nose, and short rounded ears.

Black bears have a straight profile from forehead to nose, and larger pointed ears.

Grizzly bears have long claws, measuring 2–4in (5–10cm).

Black bears have shorter claws at around 1.5in (4cm).

Remember: If attacked by a grizzly bear, be silent and play dead. If attacked by a black bear, be loud and fight back.

HOW LONG DO ANIMALS LIVE?

Questions about animal longevity are common, but near impossible to answer. What, for instance, is the average life expectancy of humans? There are so many variables. With animals our knowledge also constantly changes in relation to observational research and scientific developments.

The 1940 edition of *Compton's Pictured Encyclopedia* provided a now well-known summary of average animal ages, illustrated with a colourful 'Isotype' by Otto and Marie Neurath. At the time it was considered an authoritative, albeit broad estimation, but it is now considered factually dated.

The lifespan of a crocodile was listed as 20–25 years. We now know that saltwater crocodiles (*Crocodylus porosus*) generally live to 65, and have been known to exceed 100.

Elephants, listed as living 55–60 years, in fact live up to 70 years in Africa (*Loxodonta africana*) and Asia (*Elephas maximus*). In captivity, Asian elephant Lin Wang (1917–2003) of Taipei Zoo reached the record-breaking age of 86.

The life expectancy of whales remains a mystery. It is thought the world's largest animal, the blue whale (*Balaenoptera musculus*), lives for 80–90 years. Bowhead whales (*Balaena mysticetus*) far exceed that. In the 1980s, Inuit whalers found harpoon points which had not been used for over a century embedded in the blubber of a recent kill. Scientists studying the eye tissue of bowhead whales have since revealed that the species can reach 200. This would make them the longest living mammals on the planet.

At the time of writing, the oldest person ever recorded was Jeanne Louise Calmont (1875–1997) from France. She lived 122 years and 164 days. Her secret to longevity: olive oil, fencing, port, chocolate and cigarettes. Calmont gave up smoking at 120.

LINNAEUS SET IN ORDER

'I have fundamentally reorganised the whole field of Natural History, raising it to the height it has now attained,' wrote Swedish botanist and zoologist Carolus Linnaeus (1707–1778). 'I doubt whether anyone today could hope, without my help and guidance, to make any advance in this field.' Linnaeus was right. His intellect and influence in the natural sciences were unsurpassed in the late 18th century and his system for classifying life would continue to be used by scientists three centuries later.

A page about this pioneer on the website of the Natural History Museum explains that 'Linnaeus was driven by a lust for nature and a desire to understand how it worked'. As an empiricist he wanted to see everything with his own eyes, describing and drawing the differences and similarities of individual plants, animals and minerals. He found that there were two common problems at the time. First, there was confusion over certain species, as one plant could have many names. Second, there was the unnecessarily complex naming system for species. The tomato, for example, was a mind boggling nine-word Latinised mix: *Solanum caule inermi herbaceo, foliis pinnatis incisis, racemis simplicibus.*

Linnaeus decided to divide nature into groups based on shared physical characteristics. This led to the development of his classification system. Plants, animals and minerals became kingdoms. These were divided into divisions, then classes, then orders, then genera, and finally species. The system of taxonomy allowed all forms of life to be named and ordered.

The relative simplicity of the idea made a chaotic natural world that much easier to understand. The plant known as deadly nightshade, devil's cherries, and dwayberry, gained a new scientific name with a lineage of taxons: *Plantae, Angiosperms, Eudicots, Atserids, Solanales, Solanaceae, Atropa, Belladonna*. Linnaeus did not stop there. He simplified all scientific names into two Latin words, called the binomial name. The tomato, for example, was renamed *Solanum lycopersicum*, and deadly nightshade became *Atropa belladonna*.

The Linnaean system for classification gave natural history a common language, ensured that species identification could be achieved with accuracy, and provided much-needed order to an otherwise chaotic world.

'... there are now many many other taxons in the hierarchy, such as microphylum and infraclass, but these are of concern only to botanists and others who are paid to know them.'
—Johnson P. Johnson, *The Armchair Naturalist* (2007)

MAGPIE MYTHS

'One for sorrow, two for joy, three for a girl, four for a boy,
Five for silver, six for gold, seven for a secret, never to be told.'

Magpies have inspired superstitions, rhymes, rumours and art. In Europe they have gained a reputation as chattering birds with an eye for collecting the shiniest and most valued trinkets. Gioachino Rossini's 1817 opera *La Gazza Ladra* ('The Thieving Magpie'), in which a magpie steals a silver spoon, has helped perpetuate this myth. Solitary magpies are also seen as harbingers of doom. Legend has it the magpie was the only bird not to comfort and mourn Jesus during his crucifixion, thus becoming associated with the devil.

'Good morning Mr Magpie. How is your lady wife today?' can still be heard in parts of the UK, accompanied by a respectful salute, in an attempt to deflect the bird's sorrow and bad fortune. Yet the magpie, like everything else in the natural world, has different meanings to different people. Native American tribes, for example, used magpie feathers in ceremonial dress as a sign of fearlessness. They are known as 'birds of joy' in China, where they symbolise good fortune, and as messengers of good news in South Korea.

> 'Magpies are like poets in that they have a voice which can express words with distinct sounds, like human speech. Even if they cannot speak, they imitate the sound of the human voice. They hang from branches and chatter annoyingly.'
> —*The Bestiary of Anne Walshe* (1633)

EURASIAN OTTER FACTS

In 21st century Britain, the Eurasian otter (*Lutra lutra*) is known as a symbol of survival – a species once persecuted and threatened with extinction but subsequently legally protected and now seemingly thriving in the wild. The recolonisation of waterways by otters in every county of England has been celebrated. Yet they are not appreciated by everyone. The theft of prize-winning koi carp from garden ponds by 'cuddly killers' have hit the headlines. An increased impact on local fish stocks has also led to serious calls for a cull from sections of the fisheries community. Those who consider them pests bemoan the reintroduction of captive-bred otters for having effected the species' comeback. They remain mysterious and misunderstood creatures. Some otter facts:

1. Otters have always had a reputation as fish-killers, and rightly so – they eat fish. Historically, otter hunters were seen as experts in pest control. They protected stew ponds and inland fisheries by killing the predatory mammal. Humane management strategies including otter-proof fencing are now available.

2. When hunting for sport became increasingly popular in the 19th century, the hunted otter was not seen as a pest, but valued as a sporting quarry and preserved. Had it not been for the hunting fraternity, those with a vested interest in fish would have exterminated them from all but the wildest places.

3. In the 1960s, otter hunters were the first to discover the dramatic decrease of the otter population. They were not responsible for the decline. The cause was later proven to be polluted waterways caused by pesticides – dieldrin was the main culprit.

4. Philip Wayre of the Otter Trust (founded in 1971) was the last person to captive-breed and release Eurasian otters. One hundred and seventeen otters were reintroduced between 1983 and 1999 – that is all. None have been reintroduced since.

5. In terms of the otter population, some perspective is needed. The hedgehog, often in the news due to its declining UK population, is thought to have 1 million individuals in the wild. The badger, a carrier of TB, has an estimated population of 250,000. The red squirrel, whose survival sanctions the culling of thousands of invasive grey squirrels, has roughly 160,000 individuals. The otter has an estimated population of just 10,000.

> Of the thirteen species of otter around the world, all appear on the International Union for Conservation of Nature's Red List of Threatened Species, and their survival is by no means certain. Why not visit the International Otter Survival Fund (IOSF) website to find out how you can help.

SWIFTLET SALIVA

Birds' nests are constructed to provide warmth, incubation for eggs and a safe environment for hatchlings. White-nest swiftlets (*Aerodramus fuciphagus*), for example, take up to 35 days to build theirs in the dark caves of south-east Asia. By fastening interwoven layers of hardened saliva to the rock, they form protective translucent casings high above the cave floor. One would assume such a location would be free from danger; well, not entirely. In Chinese culture, these nests have become the most unlikely of culinary ingredients – the key component of bird's nest soup. According to legend, the delicacy was first eaten in the court of the Tang emperors (618–907). When the ruler complained there was no special taste, the imperial cook insisted it had medicinal properties, which saved his life. Historical records suggest the popular use of edible bird's nests can be traced back to the Ming Dynasty (1368–1644).

Traditional methods of harvesting saw gatherers with flaming torches scale heights of up to 300 feet on bamboo scaffolding, plucking nests from rock chambers. Although this risked human life, the reputed medicinal values of this 'white gold' made injury or death worthwhile. According to Xie Guan's (1921) *Medical Dictionary of China*, 'bird's nest' was 'used for revitalising chi, balancing chi, nourishing the lungs, improving appetite, dissolving phlegm, stopping cough, increasing sperm, nourishing bone marrow and as an aphrodisiac.' Although these healing powers have not been confirmed by modern science, the cultural importance of this natural product continues.

The birds' nest trade has become a global industry. In the mid-1990s, a kilogram – the equivalent of 120 nests – cost US$400. Today, the surge in demand in China, Hong Kong, Taiwan and the United States has meant the same weight is valued at up to $3,000. In restaurants people are willing to pay up to $100 a bowl. The commercialisation of edible nests has seen the rise of modern swiftlet farming in Malaysia, Indonesia and Thailand. Tall custom-made buildings, equipped with controlled lighting, temperature, humidity and even recordings of swiftlet song are replacing traditional cave habitats. Exporters are reaping the rewards. Indonesia made $226m in 2009. For Malaysia, the world's biggest exporter, the industry is thought to be worth a staggering $1.59bn (£1.01bn). The thought of eating swiftlet saliva may not be to everyone's taste, but with the spread of birds' nest factories, the once overexploited species may have a more secure future.

BIRD'S NEST SOUP

100g (3½oz) dried bird's nest
2 tbsp cornstarch
1.5l (2½ pints) chicken stock
whites of 2 eggs
1 large chicken breast, minced
1 tsp salt
2 spring onions, finely chopped
50g (1½oz) cooked ham, shredded

1. Soak the bird's nest overnight, then drain, rinse, and pick out any remaining pieces of foreign matter (e.g. feathers, twigs).

2. Mix the cornstarch with a little of the stock to make a paste. Set aside. Put the rest of the stock in a large saucepan and bring to the boil. Add the bird's nest and simmer for 30 minutes.

3. In a clean bowl, lightly beat the egg whites, then fold gently into the minced chicken. Add the chicken and egg white mixture to the hot soup a little at a time and return to the boil. Stir well.

4. Add the salt, then stir in the cornstarch paste to thicken the soup. Transfer to serving bowls and garnish with the spring onion and shredded ham.

A HOME AWAY FROM HOME

Many a species has been introduced to foreign lands, with seemingly good intentions. Yet certain visitors gain a reputation for becoming far too comfortable and outstaying their welcome. In Australia, grey rabbits and cane toads are two examples of guests-turned-pests. In 1859, nostalgic Englishman Thomas Austin liberated 24 grey rabbits on his farm to remind him of home. Within a decade there were over 2 million. The spot of hunting Austin craved had led to a population explosion, overgrazing, soil erosion and the loss of several indigenous species. By 1950 the number had risen to a staggering 600 million. Despite the release of the myxoma virus in that same year, the species could not be wiped out.

The arrival of the cane toad was rather less humble. Identified as pest controllers by the Australian Bureau of Sugar Experimental Stations, 102 were imported from Hawaii in 1935 to prey on cane beetle larvae that were eating the roots of sugar cane, killing the plants. The toads bred and around 3,000 were released in the sugar cane plantations of North Queensland. Ironically, these toxic toads had little impact on the pests, but were successful at multiplying and spreading at a devastating rate. By 1984 they had reached the Northern Territory and were responsible for poisoning native species and pets (cane toads exude toxin from their glands, which proves fatal when ingested), depleting native fauna, and reducing insectivore prey. In 2005, Australia's Environment Minister, Ian Campbell, labelled them 'nasty little critters'. Another MP, David Tollner, openly encouraged residents to control them the by any means; his suggestion of whacking them with cricket bats and golf clubs was particularly controversial. With the infestation showing no bounds, scientists hope the creation of genetically engineered toads carrying a daughterless gene will prove successful in the future. Today, each with respective populations of over 200 million, grey rabbits and cane toads serve as warnings of the damage alien species can have on habitats.

The moral of this story is that the introduction of species invariably disrupts the ecological balance of an environment, especially when natural predators are lacking.

> *Ecological balance* is broadly defined by
> WWF as 'a state of dynamic equilibrium
> within a community of organisms in which
> genetic, species and ecosystem diversity
> remain relatively stable, subject to gradual
> changes through natural succession.'

EXPENSIVE ALIENS

The spread of invasive alien species disrupts the natural balance of host environments, threatens the survival of native species, and reduces biodiversity. Their presence is also damaging to the global economy, costing an estimated $1.4 trillion (£913bn) a year. The United States have quoted an annual loss of $120 billion, the European Union €12.5 billion, Australia AU$7 billion and Britain over £2 billion. To see how these staggering figures start adding up, a few examples of annual costs in Great Britain are shown below:

- An estimated £160m on weed control

- £13.9m of damage caused by deer vehicle collisions (many of which were non-native species)

- £11m to eradicate rhododendron from a national park in Wales

- £10m estimated cost to British timber industry of squirrel damage to beech, sycamore and oak woodland

- £2m spent to eradicate Japanese knotweed on a 2 hectare development site

- £1m delay caused to a road development scheme while waiting to treat Japanese knotweed

- £120,000 spent by one water works on modifications to cope with zebra mussels.

Figures: GB Non-native Species Secretariat

> According to the GB Non-native Species Secretariat, Japanese knotweed costs the British economy £166 million a year. It has been estimated that £1.56 billion would be needed to fund a nationwide eradication.

MOST WANTED INVADERS

The ecological and economic damage caused by non-native plants and animals led the Environment Agency to announce the 'Top 10 Invasive Species' in 2011. The following list reveals the 'most wanted' alien invaders on British waterways:

1. Killer shrimp (*Dikerogammarus villosus*)
2. Water primrose (*Ludwigia grandiflora*)
3. Floating pennywort (*Hydrocotyle ranunculoides*)
4. American signal crayfish (*Pacifastacus leniusculus*)
5. Topmouth gudgeon (*Pseudorasbora parva*)
6. Giant hogweed (*Heracleum mantegazzianum*)
7. Japanese knotweed (*Polygonum cuspidatum*)

8. Himalayan balsam (*Impatiens glandulifera*)
9. Mink (*Neovison vison*)
10. Parrot's feather (*Myriophyllum aquaticum*)

> In Britain, the spread of the grey squirrel has been described as 'the most successful invasion since 1066'. First introduced to England in 1876, at Henbury Park, Cheshire, the fashion of deliberately releasing these 'ornamental exotics' continued for the next 60 years. The march of the North American species has seen them exceed 2 million individuals, dwarfing the indigenous red squirrel, which has an estimated population of 160,000. As immune carriers of the squirrelpox virus, a disease deadly to reds, greys have become public enemy number one in British woodlands.

EVERGLADES

During the Second Seminole War (1835–1842) an American surgeon described Florida's subtropical wetlands as 'a perfect paradise for Indians, alligators, serpents, frogs, and every other kind of loathsome reptile'. It was essentially seen as a worthless swamp. These attitudes started to change when Marjory Stoneman Douglas (1890–1998) published *The Everglades: River of Grass* in 1947. 'There are no other Everglades in the world,' Douglas wrote:

Nothing anywhere else is like them; their vast glittering openness, wider than the enormous visible round of the horizon, the racing free saltness and sweetness of their massive winds, under the dazzling blue heights of space. They are unique also in the simplicity, the diversity, the related harmony of the forms of life they enclose.

Her flowing prose portrayed the unique history and importance of the fragile ecosystem. The activism of Douglas, as founder of Friends of the Everglades, also helped restyle, preserve, protect and restore the 2 million acre 'river of grass'. Today the Everglades are promoted as a unique wildlife haven, where temperate and tropical species coexist. A million annual visitors explore once-impregnable swamps, enjoy exhilarating airboat rides, and observe alligators and crocodiles in the same waters. This does not happen anywhere else on earth.

PYTHON CHALLENGE™

Burmese pythons (*Python molurus bivittatus*) were first recorded in the Everglades in 1979. These escaped or discarded pets went on to breed, leaving Florida with an estimated population of between 30,000 and 100,000. They prey on native birds, bobcats, alligators and other native species. In 2011 a 16ft (4.9m) python was found to have a whole 76lb (34kg) deer in its stomach. The following year, *National Geographic* reported the discovery of a 'monstrous' record-breaking Burmese measuring 17.7ft (5.4m), carrying 87 eggs.

There is no question that these enormous predators

need to be controlled. Quite how is another matter. The Nature Conservancy launched the Python Patrol in 2008 to halt the spread to nearby conservation areas. State laws prohibit Burmese ownership without a federal permit. The Obama administration went one step further in 2012, banning the importation of the Burmese python, the northern and southern African pythons and the yellow anaconda. The ban was announced in a news conference at the Everglades National Park. The Interior Secretary, Ken Salazar, stated:

> It does us no good to put in these billions of dollars in investments in the Everglades only to have these giant constrictor snakes come in and undo the good that we are doing ... The action we're taking today is a milestone in the protection of the Everglades.

In December 2012 the Florida Fish and Wildlife Conservation Commission (FWC) took a more direct strategy – announcing a public hunting competition called Python Challenge™. Five cash prizes, ranging from $750 to $1,500, were up for grabs for both the general public and python harvesting permit holders. Almost 1,600 people from 38 states registered – each becoming a python hunter for a month. This attracted international interest. South African snake expert Austin Stevens voiced his concerns:

> Overwhelming numbers of feral pythons endanger native Everglades species. Unfortunately, they

need to be removed and disposed of humanely by expert catchers, and not shot to bits by gun-toting amateurs.

The official results of the challenge were announced by FWC on 18 February 2013. Between 12 January and 10 February 2013, just 68 Burmese pythons were killed. First prizes were:

$1,500 grand prize for harvesting the most Burmese pythons
General competition: Brian Barrows, harvested six
Permit holders competition: Ruben Ramirez, harvested 18

$1,000 first place prize for harvesting the longest Burmese python
General competition: Paul Shannon, 14ft 3in (4.4m) long
Permit holders competition: Ruben Ramirez, 10ft 6.8in (3.25m) long

FWC Executive Director Nick Wiley celebrated the challenge results. The goal of raising public awareness about the invasive species had been achieved. He also thanked the competitors for gathering 'invaluable information that will help refine and focus combined efforts to control pythons in the Everglades'.

This competition has certainly raised worldwide awareness of the Burmese python problem. It has also underlined the point that 'expert catchers' are required, and the fact that controlling the population will be a 'monstrous' challenge.

IS IT A BIRD OR A PLANE?

Soaring birds share the empty skies with aircraft. Occasionally their flight paths collide at great heights. On 29 November 1973 a Rüppell's griffon (*Gyps rueppellii*), a type of vulture, was sucked into an engine of a commercial aircraft at 37,000ft (12,280m) over Abijan, Ivory Coast, western Africa. The plane was damaged, though landed safely. The bird, which usually has a wingspan of 10ft (3m), was identified by its feathered remains. As the highest recorded bird strike, this unfortunate incident makes the Rüppell's griffon the highest-flying bird on the planet.

BATS: HORRORS OR HEROES?

'A bat is beautifully soft and silky,' Mark Twain (1835–1910) wrote in his autobiography. 'I do not know any creature that is pleasanter to the touch or is more grateful of caressings, if offered in the right spirit.' The American author developed his fondness for *Chiroptera* as a child. He recounts visiting a nearby cave, collecting the flying mammals and taking them home in his coat pocket, much to the alarm of his mother. 'It was remarkable, the way she couldn't learn to like private bats,' Twain pondered.

It is perhaps unsurprising that Twain's mother was not keen. Bats have long had a reputation for being loathsome and fearful. Their association with witchcraft, black magic and vampires has cast them as evil, shape-shifting symbols of death. Their appearance also does not help, as the drawings opposite by Ernst Haeckel (1834–1919) illustrate.

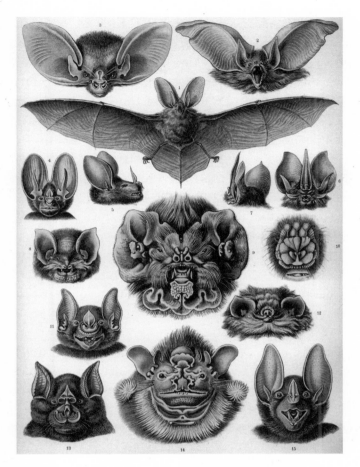

Key:

1 & 2: Brown long-eared bat (*Plecotus auritus*)
3: Lesser long-eared bat (*Nyctophilus geoffroyi geoffroyi*)
4: Lesser false vampire bat (*Megaderma spasma trifolium*)
5: Big-eared woolly bat (*Chrotopterus auritus*)
6 & 7: Tomes's sword-nosed bat (*Lonchorhina aurita*)

8: Mexican funnel-eared bat (*Natalus stramineus*)
9: Antillean ghost-faced bat (*Mormoops blainvillii*)
10: Flower-faced bat (*Anthops ornatus*)
11: Greater spear-nosed bat (*Phyllostomus hastatus*)
12: Thumbless bat (*Furipterus horrens*)
13: Greater horseshoe bat (*Rhinolophus ferrumequinum*)
14: Wrinkle-faced bat (*Centurio senex*)
15: Spectral bat (*Vampyrus spectrum*)

Despite appearances and anecdotes, they are not sinister horrors of the night, but heroes for ecosystems and the economy. Globally, bats are key insect predators. They are also important seed dispersers and pollinators for many plants. Director of the Organization for Bat Conservation, Rob Mies, is on a mission to change public perceptions. 'I try to find things that I feel people will be wowed by, that if bats didn't exist, their life would actually change,' Mies told *The Baltimore Sun*. 'For adults, I ask them if they like tequila. We take tequila from the agave plant, and the agave is only pollinated by bats.'

So the next time bats fly into conversation, avoid sinister talk of vampires and use this connection to steer the discussion on to a happier subject instead. Margarita, anyone?

Forty-seven species of bat live in the United States. The largest urban bat colony can be found at the Congress Avenue Bridge in Austin, Texas. Each summer this is home to an estimated 1.5 million Mexican free-tailed bats (*Tadarida brasiliensis*), also known as Brazilian free-tailed bats. Each night they eat an estimated 10,000–30,000lbs (4,500–13,600kg) of insects. The twilight emergence from the roost attracts over 100,000 tourists a year to the bridge.

RED HOT CHILI PEPPERS

An increased heartbeat, sweat, pain and tears are just some of the sensations experienced by heat-seeking chilli connoisseurs. The chemical responsible for giving chillies their distinctive spicy hotness is capsaicin (pronounced cap-say-sin). It works by stimulating pain-sensing nerve endings in the skin and tricking the brain into thinking they are burning.

In 1912 American pharmacist Wilbur Scoville (1865–1942) created the Scoville Organoleptic Test to measure the spiciness of chilli peppers. With this test an extract of capsaicin oil is incrementally diluted with sugar-water solution until the heat becomes undetectable. Pure capsaicin has a rating of 16,000,000 Scoville Heat Units (SHU), the equivalent of 16 million dilutions. Chilli varieties range in SHU from the sweet bell pepper (0), jalapeño (2,500–5,000), Habanero or Scotch bonnet (100,000–350,000), to the Trinidad Moruga Scorpion (2.1 million).

So why are chillies so hot? Biologist Joshua Tewksbury and his team have some answers. Chillies, like all fruit, rely on effective seed dispersal. Their intense spiciness is caused by capsaicin – this has no impact on birds, but acts as a repellent for animals not involved in this process. Another more recent discovery was that chillies in north-eastern Bolivia were not only far milder than their south-western cousins but they were more susceptible to the harmful fungal microbe *Fusarium semitectum*. The milder variety has less need for capsaicinoid protection as the fungus and feeding insects which spread

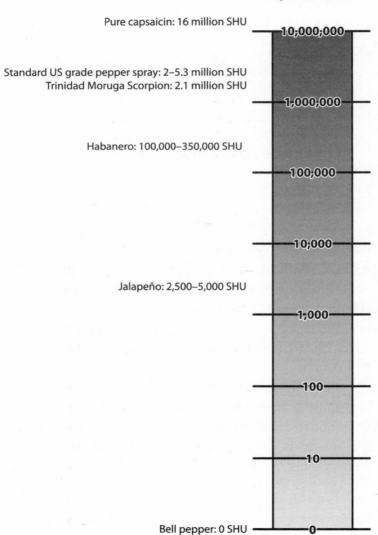

Scoville Heat Units (exponential scale)

Pure capsaicin: 16 million SHU — 10,000,000

Standard US grade pepper spray: 2–5.3 million SHU
Trinidad Moruga Scorpion: 2.1 million SHU — 1,000,000

Habanero: 100,000–350,000 SHU — 100,000

10,000

Jalapeño: 2,500–5,000 SHU — 1,000

100

10

Bell pepper: 0 SHU — 0

the microbes are rarer in that region. Undoubtedly, this ability to fend off *Fusarium semitectum* had a role in the earliest cultivation of the most eye-watering chilli peppers over 6,000 years ago.

> Are you fed up with squirrels and other animals raiding the bird feeder in your garden? Fear not. Chilli powder is the safe and effective solution. When mixed with seeds it deters mammals, leaving plenty of food for the spice-resistant birds.

KING OF FRUITS

Canned pineapple was all the rage in the 1980s – it was an exotic fruit for every occasion. Gammon with pineapple for a main meal. Pineapple upside cake made a splendid dessert. Cheese and pineapple stick appetisers graced social occasions. The fruit remains popular today due to its unique taste, convenience and culinary compatibility.

The western world first set its collective eyes on the pineapple (*Ananas comosus*) in 1493, when Christopher Columbus' second voyage landed in what is now Brazil. The discovery delighted the Spanish monarchy, as this 1516 account by Peter Martyr (1457–1526) reveals:

The most invincible King Ferdinand relates that he has eaten another fruit brought from those countries. It is like a pine-net in form and colour, covered with scales, and firmer than a melon. Its flavour excels all other fruits. This fruit, which the King prefers to all others, does not grow upon a tree but upon a plant, similar to an artichoke or an acanthus ... Spaniards who have eaten them fresh plucked where they grow, speak with the highest appreciation of their delicate flavour.

In *The Pineapple: King of Fruits* (2006), historian Fran Beauman explains it was this early seal of approval which cast the exotic oddity on the world stage as worthy of royalty. Its reputation continued to grow. In 1629, Dutch physician Jacobus Bontius stated, 'There is not a nobler fruit in the universe.' Charles II of England used the fruit as a powerful public relations tool in 1668 when holding a banquet in honour of the French ambassador. Alongside its rarity and high value, it represented England's colonial power in the West Indies. The fruit was confirmed as a status symbol when Charles II commissioned a portrait of himself being presented with a pineapple by the royal gardener John Rose.

In the following centuries the fruit became a must-have accessory for the upper classes. They were grown in gardens, appeared in paintings and informed architectural designs. The Dunmore Pineapple, one of the architectural wonders of Scotland, is a fine example.

Even by the mid-20th century the fruit had royal connections. In 1947, 500 cases of canned pineapple were sent to the future Queen Elizabeth II as a wedding gift from the Australian government.

Perhaps unsurprisingly, the pineapple is not alone in vying for the 'king of fruits' title. In south-east Asia that honour is bestowed to the durian, a fruit more commonly known by the associated phrase, 'tastes like heaven but smells like hell'. The butter-coloured flesh beneath the thorn-covered husks is all important. Alfred Russell Wallace (1823–1913) described the heavenly flavours as follows:

> A rich custard highly flavoured with almonds gives the best general idea of it, but there are occasional wafts of flavour that call to mind cream-cheese, onion-sauce, sherry-wine, and other incongruous dishes. Then there is a rich glutinous smoothness in the pulp which nothing else possesses, but which adds to its delicacy.

The odour of raw durian, on the other hand, is so pungent that it is now generally banned in hotels and on public transport in Singapore. According to food writer Richard Sterling it is 'best described as pig-shit, turpentine and onions, garnished with a gym sock'. If this is not offensive enough, American chef Anthony Bourdain warns durian eaters, 'Your breath will smell as if you'd been French-kissing your dead grandmother.'

So which is really the rightful owner of the king of fruits crown? It is, of course, a matter of taste. I am not sure about you, but personally those unappetising descriptions of the durian have convinced me that the pineapple is king.

'No durians!' In parts of Asia, signs bearing this symbol can be seen in many public places.

> Pineapples are the only known source of bromelain, the protein-digesting enzyme which essentially eats flesh. This is what leaves that tingling sensation in your mouth when enjoying the fruit. The chemical is used to tenderise meat, and is one of the reasons pineapple is coupled with gammon when cooking. In the 1980s, Judy Mazel (1943–2007) made millions from the 'Beverly Hills Diet', a weight-loss craze which revolved around eating a lot of pineapple.

BATHROOM FRUIT

My favourite fruit has got to be the mango (*Mangifera indica*), for its sweet taste and smell, its soft but pulpy texture, the juices that drip down your face and arms. It really brings out the child in me – what other fruit can be sliced, turned inside out, and presented as a hedgehog?

As the national fruit of India, Pakistan and the Philippines, mangoes are not short of admirers. According to legend, Manu (the progenitor of mankind) asked Brahma (the Hindu god of creation) to create a fruit for everyone: 'Lord! grant us a fruit full of sweet juice, which has the fragrance of flowers, sweetness of fruits and nutrition of cereals. Also, let it be accessible to all, rich and poor.' Brahma agreed, pouring drops from his kamandal; mango groves later sprouted there.

The fruit has been enjoyed by the masses for over 4,000 years and celebrated in Indian art, poetry and literature. During the British Raj, the colonists over-looked this cultural value, instead focusing on the excessive juiciness and associated mango-eating etiquette. Renowned for their rigid Victorian virtues, the British did not enjoy the sight of Indians sucking on mangoes with juice dripping all over the floor. Dr M.S. Randhawa (1909–1988) observed that the British would insist that the Indian staff in their houses only eat mangoes in the bathroom. The mango's somewhat derogatory tag of 'bathroom fruit' was born.

TRUFFLES

French food writer Jean Anthelme Brillat-Savarin (1755–1826) once described this subterranean mushroom as the 'diamond of the kitchen'. The Burgundy truffle (*tuber uncinatum*), Perigord black truffle (*tuber melanosporum*) and white truffle (*tuber magnatum*) remain as highly prized today.

The average prices per kilo in 2009 were £290 (US$430) for Burgundy truffles, £900 (US$1,300) for black truffles and £2,800 (US$4,200) for white truffles. The expense and allure of this mysterious fungus is informed by its rarity and origin. All truffle species have a symbiotic relationship with the roots of suitable host trees. Growing beneath the ground, they are near impossible to track down. Unless, that is, you are a truffle hog.

A truffle hog is a domestic pig with the innate ability to smell and seek truffles. It is thought that sows are attracted to a compound within the fungus which resembles the sex pheromone of boar saliva, androstenol. Trufflers have taken advantage of this since Roman times. The drawback with this animal is its desire to eat the prized fungus, and the damage it causes to truffle's mycelia during digging, which reduces future harvests. For these reasons, the use of the hog to hunt truffles has been prohibited in Italy since 1985. Trained hogs are still used in the United States and in other parts of Europe.

The alternative truffle-hunting companion is the truffle dog. Lagotto Romagnolo are recognised for sniffing out truffles, but most breeds could be trained for this role. They are said to be far easier to control.

Macau casino owner Stanley Ho parted with the largest sum ever paid for a single truffle. The white truffle, which weighed 1.5kg (3.3lb), sold at auction for an astonishing £165,000 (US$330,000) in 2007.

DAFFODILS

As a major figure in the Romantic movement, English poet William Wordsworth (1770–1850) found inspiration through a personal connection with nature. Wordsworth's poem 'I Wandered Lonely as a Cloud' (also known as 'Daffodils') is the perfect example. Those famous words about daffodils 'fluttering and dancing in the breeze', however, did not immediately enter his mind, nor were they all his own. In fact, he had not even been alone. The daffodils were first experienced during a walk he shared with his sister Dorothy in April 1802. Dorothy recorded the following thoughts in her diary:

> When we were in the woods beyond Gowbarrow Park, we saw a few daffodils close to the water side [...] I never saw daffodils so beautiful they grew among the mossy stones about and about them, some rested their heads upon these stones as on a pillow for weariness and the rest tossed and reeled and danced and seemed as if they verily laughed with the wind that blew upon them over the lake, they looked so gay ever dancing ever changing.

It was not until two years later that William penned what would become his most popular work. William's wife Mary also deserves some praise. The lines 'They flash upon that inward eye, Which is the bliss of solitude', considered by many as the best in the poem, were hers. Daffodils became even more poignant to the Wordsworth family after the death of their daughter in

1847. The grief-stricken parents planted hundreds of bulbs on their land, naming the area Dora's Field in her memory. As the poem continues to bring pleasure to generations of readers, this 'host of golden daffodils' in Rydal village can still be found 'fluttering and dancing' every spring.

I wandered lonely as a cloud
That floats on high o'er vales and hills,
When all at once I saw a crowd,
A host, of golden daffodils;
Beside the lake, beneath the trees,
Fluttering and dancing in the breeze.

Continuous as the stars that shine
And twinkle on the milky way,
They stretched in never-ending line
Along the margin of a bay:
Ten thousand saw I at a glance,
Tossing their heads in sprightly dance.

The waves beside them danced; but they
Out-did the sparkling waves in glee:
A poet could not but be gay,
In such a jocund company:
I gazed—and gazed—but little thought
What wealth the show to me had brought:

For oft, when on my couch I lie
In vacant or in pensive mood,
They flash upon that inward eye
Which is the bliss of solitude;
And then my heart with pleasure fills,
And dances with the daffodils.

OH, BEE HIVE!

Bees seem to have such an easy life. They buzz around on sunny days, find beautiful flowers, rub their legs on pollen, buzz around some more, and make honey. In reality their lives are far more regimented. Worker bees not only know their place in the hive, they must also act their age. The duties of an adult are as follows:

Day 1–2: Clean cells and keep the brood warm

Day 3–5: Feed older larvae

Day 6–11: Feed youngest larvae

Day 12–17: Produce wax, build comb, carry food, ripen honey

Day 18–22: Guard the hive entrance

Day 23+: Fly from hive, pollinate plants, collect pollen, nectar and water

SEVEN NATURAL WONDERS

In 1997 the television network CNN announced its 'Seven Wonders of the Natural World'. As well as the requirement that each be totally unique, characteristics such as height, width, volume, beauty and amazement were all taken into account. The wonders were:

Aurora (Northern and Southern Lights)
The unpredictability of these phenomena were judged to add to the wonderment.

Grand Canyon, Arizona, USA

Although not the deepest or longest canyon in the world, the scale, beauty and accessibility of this natural environment forced this wonder onto the list.

Great Barrier Reef, north-eastern coast of Australia

The assemblage of over 2,900 separate reefs makes this the largest coral reef system in the world. Covering 133,000 square miles (344,000km^2) the reef can be seen from outer space.

Harbour of Rio de Janiero, Brazil

The world's largest bay, surrounded by Sugar Loaf Mountain, Corcovado Peak and the hills of Tijuca.

Mount Everest, Himalaya Mountains, Nepal and Tibet

The highest mountain on earth, with a summit reaching 29,029ft (8,848m).

Paricutin Volcano, Michoacán, Mexico

The birth of this cinder cone volcano was witnessed by a Mexican farmer in February 1943 – this event was judged to differentiate the young volcano from all others. It grew to 1,100ft (335m) in one year, continued erupting until 1952, and now stands at 9,210ft (2,800m).

Victoria Falls, Zambia and Zimbabwe

The largest waterfall on the planet based on width (1.7km/1.1 mile) and height (360ft/108m).

The Seven Natural Wonders organisation continues to promote this original list, encouraging people to visit, explore and engage with them. On the organisation's website (sevennaturalwonders.org) votes can also be cast for the official natural wonders of each continent.

NEW7WONDERS OF NATURE

'If we want to save anything, we first need to truly appreciate it' was the slogan that fronted the New7Wonders of Nature campaign between 2007 and 2011. Conscious that the original seven wonders had stolen the show from other natural phenomena, initiative founder Bernard Weber was keen to put less familiar wonders on the map. Recognising that 'competition and the fear of losing something special' motivated individuals, he decided this list should be determined by a global poll. One hundred million votes later, these seven wonders made up the new alternative list:

1. Amazon rainforest and river, Bolivia, Brazil, Colombia, Ecuador, French Guiana, Guyana, Peru, Suriname and Venezuela
2. Halong Bay, Vietnam
3. Iguazu/Iguaçu Falls (National Park), Argentina, Brazil
4. Jeju Island, South Korea
5. Komodo Island (National Park), Indonesia
6. Puerto Princesa Underground River, Philippines
7. Table Mountain (National Park), South Africa

The 28 finalists certainly benefited from this four-year campaign, but the new list is controversial. The telephone and SMS poll did not prevent repeat votes, leaving it open to claims that government-led voting could have shaped the list. Whether or not this was the case, the fact that it is still being talked about maintains an appreciation of these wonders on a global scale.

DANGER

When people sense danger they have a rush of adrenaline, the heart beats faster, and the body prepares itself for 'fight or flight'. On occasion, those not blessed with fighting spirit or natural pace may look to the animal world and think, if only. Opossums famously play dead and skunks release a pungent spray which can temporarily blind and debilitate those on the receiving end.

More drastic defence mechanisms also prove useful. The hairy frog intentionally breaks its own toe bones, which pierce through the skin to reveal sharp retractable claws. Horned lizards boast another comic-book-like ability. By pressuring their sinus cavities, vessels burst, allowing blood to be sprayed at predators from their own eyes. The sea cucumber takes it to the next level, violently shooting toxic internal organs out of its anus. It literally turns itself inside out to stay alive.

As extreme, even disgusting, as the options are, one cannot but feel respect for such strong survival instincts.

> 'Hail to thee, Nature, thou parent of all things!'
> —Pliny the Elder, *Naturalis Historia*, AD77

SCHMIDT STING PAIN INDEX

Anyone unlucky enough to have been stung by an insect knows it can be painful. But have you ever wondered how much it really hurts, and what that pain was like in relation to other stings? Experienced entomologist Justin O. Schmidt has been at the sharp end of bees, wasps and ants throughout his career. Where most people would moan about the experience, Schmidt used his personal research to create a relative pain scale index. After seeing Schmidt's scale, your own sting experience may not seem as painful as you first thought.

1.0 Sweat bee: Light, ephemeral, almost fruity. A tiny spark has singed a single hair on your arm.

1.2 Fire ant: Sharp, sudden, mildly alarming. Like walking across a shag carpet and reaching for the light switch.

1.8 Bullhorn acacia ant: A rare, piercing, elevated sort of pain. Someone has fired a staple into your cheek.

2.0 Bald-faced hornet: Rich, hearty, slightly crunchy. Similar to getting your hand mashed in a revolving door.

2.0 Yellowjacket: Hot and smoky, almost irreverent. Imagine W.C. Fields extinguishing a cigar on your tongue.

3.0 Red harvester ant: Bold and unrelenting. Somebody is using a drill to excavate your ingrown toenail.

3.0   Paper wasp: Caustic and burning. Distinctly bitter aftertaste. Like spilling a beaker of hydrochloric acid on a paper cut.

4.0   Pepsis wasp: Blinding, fierce, shockingly electric. A running hair dryer has been dropped into your bubble bath (if you get stung by one you might as well lie down and scream).

4.0+ Bullet ant: Pure, intense, brilliant pain. Like walking over flaming charcoal with a 3-inch nail in your heel.

FEAR

As well as inspiring wonder and awe, nature is the source of irrational, uncontrollable fear. One of the most common examples is zoophobia, or the fear of animals. The most unlikely of individuals have fallen into this category. Napoleon Bonaparte, Adolf Hitler and Benito Mussolini shared a fear of cats (ailurophobia). Walt Disney, the creator of Mickey Mouse, was scared of mice (musophobia). Alfred Hitchcock, whose 1963 film *The Birds* terrified ornithophobics, hated eggs (ovophobia).

The mere thought of certain natural phenomena also makes many shudder. Clouds (nephophobia), forests (hylophobia), lakes (limnophobia), looking up (anablephobia), open high places (aeroacrophobia), plants (botanophobia), running water (potamophobia), snow (chionophobia), waves (kymophobia), and wind (ancraophobia) have all been known to strike panic and terror into sections of society.

MOST DISLIKED ANIMALS

From 1956 to 1967 the BBC broadcast the pioneering children's television series *Zootime*. Its host, the zoologist, animal behaviourist and artist Dr Desmond Morris, introduced a wide variety of exotic animals into people's homes for the first time through this medium. He also studied viewers' reactions to the on-screen animals.

The children watching *Zootime* were asked three questions: Which animal do you like the most? Which animal do you dislike the most? Please suggest a possible future item for *Zootime*. Viewers were told a prize would be given for the most interesting answer to the third question. About 50,000 children responded. A random sample of 4,200 cards were analysed and the competition results transmitted in April 1961. The top ten of most *disliked* animals was as follows:

1. Snake
2. Spider
3. Crocodile
4. Lion
5. Rat
6. Skunk
7. Gorilla
8. Rhinoceros
9. Hippopotamus
10. Tiger

The snake clearly topped the list, with one in three children choosing it as their least favoured animal. 'These were children living in a country where there is a greater chance of being struck by lightning than of being killed by a venomous snake,' Morris noted in his autobiography *Watching: Encounters with Humans and Other Animals* (2006). These dislikes are informed by phobias, appearance and unfamiliarity.

During a 2013 interview with *Practical Reptile Keeping* magazine Morris explained:

> There may be an inborn element in these phobias, but this is exaggerated by cultural influences. Very young children are not frightened of spiders or snakes. It is only when they are a little older that they change their attitudes, suggesting that perhaps their parents' teachings have had an impact.

He also acknowledged the increased influence of television on attitudes to animals:

> My old friend Sir David Attenborough has probably done more than anyone else to defend and promote reptiles. His series *Life in Cold Blood*, broadcast in 2008, went into great detail on the subject.

It would be fascinating to see if attitudes have changed after half a century. Would children choose the same animal as most disliked in 21st-century Britain? How much would such a list differ if compiled in other countries?

VENOM

Whatever anyone says, venomous snakes are scary. With just one strike, those hypodermic fangs can pierce the skin, deliver venom and take life or limb. Around the world an estimated 5.5 million snake bites cause between 90,000 and 125,000 deaths a year. Mark O'Shea's authoritative guide *Venomous Snakes of the World* (2005) explains how the composition and effects of venom vary considerably. Venom can be broadly divided into:

1. **Cardiotoxins**, which lead to direct cardiotoxicity (heart damage).

2. **Coagulants**:
    - Anticoagulants cause an inability of the blood to coagulate.
    - Procoagulants cause clotting but the body repeatedly breaks down the clots until the fibrinogen in the blood is removed. The result is incoagulable blood.

3. **Cytotoxins**, which cause local swelling and tissue damage.

4. **Haemorrhagins**, which disturb the integrity of blood vessels, causing bleeding.

5. **Haemotoxins**, which lead to the breakdown of living red blood cells (haemolysis).

6. **Myotoxins**, which cause muscle breakdown (rhabdomyolysis).

7. **Nephrotoxins**, which cause kidney damage, a consequence of which can be renal failure.

8. **Neurotoxins**, a diverse group of toxins with paralytic effects:
    - Postsynaptic neurotoxins block the synaptic receptor sites. Antivenom can reverse this kind of paralysis.

- Presynaptic neurotoxins destroy the transmitter synaptic sites. This paralysis cannot be reversed with antivenom. Intubation is required to maintain life.

9. **Sarafotoxins**, which cause the narrowing of blood vessels (found only in burrowing asps of Afro-Arabia).

Of the venomous snake families, *Elapidae* have many famous species, including taipan, tiger, cobra, mamba, brown, coral, kraits and sea snakes. It is a snake of the *Elapidae* family, the inland taipan, that is judged the most venomous land snake on the planet – that is, if you go by its lethal dosage (LD50) value. At 0,02mg/kg, it is 50 times more venomous than the common cobra. One bite can potentially kill up to 100 people, and can cause cardiac arrest, respiratory failure, muscle paralysis, and potential death in less than one hour. In its native Australia, however, no fatalities have been recorded, unlike the cobra, which takes tens of thousands of lives in Asia every year.

Members of the *Viperidae* family, adders, bushmasters, rattlesnakes and vipers, have the most highly developed mechanism for delivering painful and potent venom. Their long-hinged fangs penetrate deeply and myotoxic venom eats away at the flesh.

The largest snake family, *Colubridae*, are the least dangerous, partly as many species deliver venom from elongated grooved teeth at the back of the upper jaw (Opisthoglyphous) – a less efficient mode of envenomation. Yet there are exceptions to the rule. American herpetologist Karl Schmidt was bitten by a juvenile boomslang at the Chicago Field Museum in 1957. Twenty-eight hours later he was dead.

> 'While it is true that snake venoms as a whole can cause human death, scientists today are probing deeper into the possibilities of snake venom fractions being used in medical advancements in such fields as cancer research ... Mankind has yet to learn that nature, in all its forms, needs only to be respected, not feared!'
>
> —Austin J. Stevens, *The Last Snake Man*, 2007

10 'DEADLIEST' SNAKES

There is much debate between herpetologists over what should be regarded as the deadliest snake. The 'most deadly' question also frustrates many a quiz goer, as lists are invariably subjective.

When Steve Irwin (1962–2006) went face to face with an inland taipan (also known as the 'fierce snake') he told *The Ten Deadliest Snakes in the World* (1998) viewers, 'The deadliest snake on earth came up and gave me a lick. Good thing she didn't like the taste much.'

Venomous Snakes of the World author Mark O'Shea emphasised the difficulty of separating the most deadly and most dangerous in 2007:

> Any highly venomous snake is dangerous if it bites you, irrelevant of whether it is the most venomous or the one responsible for most deaths, only one bite matters at that time, the one you just received

... I regard the most dangerous snake I have encountered to be the Sri Lankan Russell's viper which featured in my film *Venom* [2002].

Wildlife presenter and author Steve Backshall also awarded the title of 'most deadly snake in the world' to the Russell's viper in his 2007 book *Venom*.

The black mamba (*Dendroaspis polylepis*) is another example of subjectivity, in this case on a cultural scale. In 2013 a *National Geographic* contributor wrote, 'African myths exaggerate their capabilities to legendary proportions. For these reasons, the black mamba is widely considered the world's deadliest snake.'

Statistical errors have also informed 'deadliest' lists. The National Health Profile of India reported that the country had had just 1,400 snakebite mortalities in 2008. A groundbreaking project on 'Snake Mortality in India' has since found this to be a massive underestimation. Rom Whitaker explained the findings of his collaborative research on a BBC *Natural World* documentary, *One Million Snake Bites* (2011):

The results of the million death study have revealed that close to 50,000 people die from snakebite every year in India and that's out of perhaps over a million snakebites. Now there's no more denying that snakebite is a serious problem. It has reached almost epidemic proportions.

The subjectivity of deadly snake rankings led experts at the Reptile Gardens, South Dakota, USA, to compile a 'more objective' list, using their own International Danger Quotient method. On this scale, six critical factors are used to award relative marks from 1 (low) to 5 (high). The higher the total, the more deadly the ranking. Below are what they consider to be the ten deadliest snakes, in reverse order.

West African carpet viper (*Echis ocellatus*), Africa
Average size: 1; Venom yield: 1; Venom toxicity: 5; Fang length: 2; Disposition/Attitude: 5; Bites per year: 5; Total score: 19

King brown snake (*Pseudechis austalis*), Australia
Average size: 4; Venom yield: 5; Venom toxicity: 2; Fang length: 3; Disposition/Attitude: 3; Bites per year: 2; Total score: 19

Black mamba (*Dendroaspis polylepis*), Africa
Average size: 4; Venom yield: 3; Venom toxicity: 3; Fang length: 2; Disposition/Attitude: 5; Bites per year: 3; Total score: 20

Common lancehead (*Bothrops atrox*), Central/South America
Average size: 3; Venom yield: 3; Venom toxicity: 2; Fang length: 4; Disposition/Attitude: 5; Bites per year: 4; Total score: 21

King cobra (*Ophiophagus hannah*), Asia
Average size: 5; Venom yield: 5; Venom toxicity: 3; Fang length: 3; Disposition/Attitude: 3; Bites per year: 2; Total score: 21

Russell's viper (*Daboia russelii*), Asia
Average size: 3; Venom yield: 3; Venom toxicity: 3; Fang length: 3; Disposition/Attitude: 4; Bites per year: 5; Total score: 21

Coastal taipan (*Oxyuranus scutellatus*), Australia
Average size: 4; Venom yield: 3; Venom toxicity: 5; Fang length: 3; Disposition/Attitude: 4; Bites per year: 2; Total score: 22

Terciopelo (*Bothrops asper*), Central/South America
Average size: 4; Venom yield: 4; Venom toxicity: 2; Fang length: 4;
Disposition/Attitude: 5; Bites per year: 4; Total score: 23

Puff adder (*Bitis arietans*), Africa
Average size: 3; Venom yield: 4; Venom toxicity: 3; Fang length: 4;
Disposition/Attitude: 4; Bites per year: 5; Total score: 23

Papuan taipan (*Oxyuranus s. canni*), Papua New Guinea
Average size: 4; Venom yield: 3; Venom toxicity: 5; Fang length: 3;
Disposition/Attitude: 5; Bites per year: 3; Total score: 23

But wait, quiz goers, for this is not the final word on the subject. Although this list is an admirable attempt at objectivity, it is not universally accepted by other experts. Leading snake expert Mark O'Shea makes a number of dissenting comments:

- On the king brown snake: 'I would think a 6m king cobra can inject more venom than a king brown snake, I don't think it should be on the list.'

- On the black mamba: 'I also don't think I would put ... black mamba in the list of deadliest snakes – they feature so infrequently in snakebite fatalities. High chance of death following a bite is true, but few bites in the grand scheme of things.'

- On the king cobra: 'Large, emotive well-known venomous snakes end up on the list while lesser known species are missed even though they cause more deaths. King cobras are considered dangerous killers but apart from in Burma they may not feature highly being secret deep forest snakes.'

- On the coastal taipan: 'Two to three people die of snakebite in Australia each year, despite the claims that most if not all of the most venomous (I avoid the word deadly) snakes live there. People are bitten and they receive excellent medical care and survive.'

- On the puff adder: 'I would disagree that puff adders kill more people than any other African snake, they are the most widespread medically important snake but they have a relatively low kill rate per incident.'

The title of deadliest snake is difficult to bestow. What can be said with certainty is that venom should be respected; envenomators admired from afar, and close encounters left to our herpetological heroes.

'Deadly could apply to: a) snakes that have the capacity to kill, but for some reason (docility, remote distribution, rarity) don't kill anybody, or b) snakes with a proven record of taking human life.

I would say group a) are the most venomous snakes in the world and group b) are the most dangerous snakes in the world.'
—Mark O'Shea

SNAP!

'Crikey! Did you see that croc? What a beauty!' Steve Irwin (1962–2006), the self-styled crocodile hunter, will forever be associated with crocodilians. His ebullient style and hands-on approach reinvigorated the wild-life documentary genre and redirected the attention of over 500 million viewers to the plight of a previously unpopular species. He was, as David Bellamy OBE noted, one of the few of his generation who 'mixed damn good science with showbusiness'.

The influence of Irwin on crocodilian conservation is widely recognised, the difference between crocodiles and alligators rather less so. Can you identify the croco-dile below? Have a closer inspection. Careful: not too close, they bite. Is it:

U

or

V

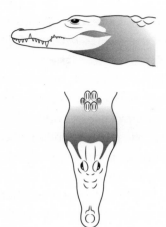

U or V? The jaw and teeth are the main clues. One has a shovel-like, U-shaped snout, the other has a sharper, V-shaped snout. The U-shaped jaw hides most teeth when the mouth is closed. The V-shaped jaw reveals the fourth tooth from the lower row.

U or V? Here's a clue. Think of the well-known rhymes 'See **U** later alligator' and 'Ne**V**er smile at a crocodile.'

U is alligator. V is crocodile.

> The term crocodilians refers to all members of the *Crocodylidae* (true crocodiles), *Alligatoridae* (alligators and caimans) and *Gavialidae* (gharial) families. At present there are 23 recognised species; the IUCN lists six as critically endangered. Crocodiles generally live in saltwater habitats, while alligators, caimans and gharials prefer freshwater.

SPEAKING UP FOR SHARKS

When it comes to conservation, pioneering work often ensures that certain names become forever associated with a species. Dian Fossey, Jane Goodall, George and Joy Adamson, Gavin Maxwell, Peter Benchley and Steve Irwin, for example, each respectively changed attitudes towards gorillas, chimpanzees, lions, otters, sharks and crocodiles. Of all those names, Peter Benchley, author of *Jaws*, the bestselling book on which the movie of the same name was based, may seem out of place. He was, of course, responsible for instilling shark phobia (selachaphobia) into generations of audiences, and turning the great white shark into the oceans' public enemy number one. But this is not a mistake. Benchley became full of guilt and regret over his man-eating creation. 'My research for the book was thorough and good, for the time,' he later said. 'I read papers, watched all the documentaries, talked to all the experts. I realise now, though, that I was very much a prisoner of traditional conceptions. And misconceptions ... Knowing what I know now, I could never write that book today. Sharks don't target human beings, and they certainly don't hold grudges.' With his very public change of heart, Benchley became an influential ocean conservationist, campaigning for the protection of sharks. His pivotal role was recognised after his death in 2006, when the Shark Research Institute inaugurated The Peter Benchley Shark Conservation Awards.

AMBERGRIS

'Whale-Waste Find', 'Floating Gold', 'Whale Vomit, Worth $60,000 Discovered'. Whenever a hardened lump of ambergris is found washed up on a beach, the story hits the headlines. The mysterious waxy substance, prized by perfume makers for centuries, continues to stimulate the senses and capture the imagination. But what exactly is it? The process which creates ambergris starts in the digestive system of sperm whales. Squid and other shellfish are broken down by acids and nematodes in the second stomach. Irritation from indigestible beaks leads to biliary secretion in the intestines, and a chemical reaction. Expelled into the ocean, usually in faecal matter, the substance has yet to develop its sweet, refined scent. Ambergris, like cheese or fine wine, needs time to mature. Over the months, years, even decades, it floats on the sea water becoming oxidised, hardened, lighter in colour and increasingly desirable. Although puns on the theme of 'Moby Sick' can raise a smile, the fragrance which has long anointed the skin of the wealthy is better described as 'preternaturally hardened dung'.

As we are on the subject of the fragrant aroma of dung, the most expensive coffee comes from beans which have travelled through the digestive system of elephants. Yes, elephants. Known as Black Ivory, the coffee is produced in northern Thailand and valued at US$1,100 (£685) per kg. So if you are looking for a 'very smooth' beverage which 'lacks the bitterness of a regular coffee' this could be for you. A little advice, at about US$50 (£31) a cup, make sure you enjoy it.

HEAVENLY DEW

The origin of pearls, the only gem made by a living animal, long baffled ancient civilisations. The Chinese believed they were the tears, variously, of sharks, dragons and mermaids. The Romans looked to the heavens. In *Naturalis Historia* (AD77), Pliny the Elder confidently wrote:

> Pearls are the offspring of shells similar to oysters; at the breeding season, the shells gape open and become filled with a dew from the sky that makes them pregnant. The quality of the pearl depends on the quality of the dew received, and on the state of the sky: a clear sky produces a clear pearl, but a cloudy sky produces a pale pearl. If the shells are well fed, the pearls grow, but if there is lightning or thunder the shells close up in fear, and so shrink from lack of food.

Today, the widely accepted explanation is far less romantic. Contrary to popular belief, sand and other foreign bodies are not the intrusive nuclei of pearl formation. Pearls, or at least the naturally formed ones, are mainly the by-product of parasitic worms. Having entered the mollusc, the intruder dies and becomes coated in conchiolin. Once hardened, further secretions then cover it with thin layers of nacreous aragonite. These glamorous status symbols are essentially the tombs of parasitic worms.

The most famous pearl in the world is La Peregrina. Discovered off the Pearl Islands in the Gulf of Panama over 500 years ago, owners have included European monarchs and Hollywood icon Dame Elizabeth Taylor. In December 2011, a Cartier necklace with La Peregrina as its centrepiece was auctioned at Christie's in New York. It sold for a record $11.8 million.

THE BIRTH AND DEATH OF AN ISLAND

At the end of June 1831 sailors reported some strange happenings in the Strait of Sicily. There was turbulence and convulsions in the bubbling waters. Thousands of dead fish floated to the surface. In July a strong foul odour reached the nearby town of Sciacca, a column of smoke billowed from the sea, there was talk of a sea monster rising from the depths. By 17 July, the mystery finally revealed itself in the form of a small volcanic island. An explosive display of fire and lava flow continued. With every eruption the island grew, reaching 4,800 metres (15,700 feet) in circumference and 63 metres (207 feet) in height.

With a prime location between Sicily and Tunisia the new island was hot property. As James Hamilton explains in *Volcano* (2012), 'it became the most picked-over piece of real estate in the Mediterranean'. The British Navy soon arrived to plant their flag. They named it Graham Island, after the First Lord of the Admiralty, Sir James Graham. Recognising the strategic value of the land, the new Bourbon King of the Two Sicilies, Ferdinand II, sent a fleet to claim ownership of the island. The Union Jack was removed, new colours planted and the island was named Ferdinandea in his honour.

The dispute over sovereignty did not end there. France and Spain also waded in. The *tricolore* of France arrived with geologist Constant Prévost, who named it Île Julia, after its July birth. The Spanish christened the island Corrao. For five months there was diplomatic tension, patriotic hysteria in the press, and naval posturing. The coming together of war fleets seemed inevitable. That is, until 17 December 1832; the day the island disappeared back into the ocean.

WE ARE NOT ALONE

World population: 7 billion. Earth is a crowded place. As a destructive and selfish species, humanity often overlooks the other organisms that live on and share our planet. In 2010 the International Union for the Conservation of Nature (IUCN) described 1,740,330 species.

CATEGORY	SPECIES
Vertebrate animals	
Mammals	5,490
Birds	9,998
Reptiles	9,084
Amphibians	6,433
Fishes	31,300
Total vertebrates	*62,305*

CATEGORY	SPECIES
Invertebrate animals	
Insects	1,000,000
Spiders and scorpions	102,248
Molluscs	85,000
Crustaceans	47,000
Corals	2,175
Others	68,827
Total invertebrates	*1,305,250*
Plants	
Flowering plants (angiosperms)	281,821
Conifers (gymnosperms)	1,021
Ferns and horsetails	12,000
Mosses	16,236
Red and green algae	10,134
Total plants	*321,212*
Others	
Lichens	17,000
Mushrooms	31,496
Brown algae	3,067
Total others	*51,563*
TOTAL SPECIES	**1,740,330**

* Domestic animals and single-celled bacteria are not included.

> 'In our hearts, we hope we never discover everything.'
> —E.O. Wilson

BATS IN BRITAIN

When former Black Sabbath vocalist Ozzy Osbourne bit off the head of a live bat at his 'Night of the Living Dead' tour of the United States in 1981, the world got the impression that Ozzy was the devil incarnate. Time has proved that this is not the case. The head-biting incident was a case of mistaken identity – he thought the bat thrown on to the stage was a plastic toy.

Bats in Ozzy's UK homeland can nonetheless be reassured that any repeat of such antics will not be tolerated – the seventeen breeding species are fully protected by law, as are their roosts. Alongside the Bat Conservation Trust, there are also nearly 100 local bat groups.

The largest bat that appears in Britain also happens to be the rarest. It is the greater mouse-eared bat (*Myotis myotis*). It was declared extinct on these shores in 1990 but several individuals have been sighted since. At present there is thought be a solitary male, which has hibernated at the same site in Sussex since 2002.

Globally, there are 1,116 bat species, accounting for 20 per cent of all terrestrial mammals. A quarter of the world's bats are threatened with extinction. These are traditionally split into *Megachiroptera* (megabats) *Microchiroptera* (microbats, echolocating bats). Habitat destruction, disease and persecution threaten the survival of these misunderstood creatures.

OTTER SPOTTING IN BRITAIN

Otter spotting is notoriously unpredictable. It requires planning, patience and a lot of luck. The possibility of getting a rare glimpse during an afternoon stroll beside the river is unlikely. However, chances do improve if you visit watery environments where previous sightings have been made, at dusk or dawn.

The Wildlife Trusts recently assisted future otter spotters by suggesting 'Great places to look for otters', listing 34 sites across the UK:

1. Cricklepit Mill (Devon Wildlife Trust)
2. Essex Nightwatch (Essex Wildlife Trust)
3. Smallbrook Meadows (Wiltshire Wildlife Trust)
4. Aughton Woods (Lancashire Wildlife Trust)
5. Gilfach Farm (Radnorshire Wildlife Trust)
6. Winnall Moors (Hants and Isle of Wight Wildlife Trust)
7. Portrack Marsh (Tees Valley Wildlife Trust)
8. Staveley (Yorkshire Wildlife Trust)
9. Falls of Clyde (Scottish Wildlife Trust)
10. Glenarm Nature Reserve (Ulster Wildlife Trust)
11. Magor Marsh (Gwent Wildlife Trust)
12. Wolseley Centre (Staffordshire Wildlife Trust)
13. Westhay Moor (Somerset Wildlife Trust)
14. The Knapp & Papermill (Worcestershire Wildlife Trust)
15. Teifi Marshes – The Welsh Wildlife Centre (Wildlife Trust of South & West Wales)
16. Balloo Wetland (Ulster Wildlife Trust)
17. Loch of the Lowes (Scottish Wildlife Trust)
18. Spey Bay (Scottish Wildlife Trust)

19. Lower Test Nature Reserve (Hants and Isle of Wight Wildlife Trust)
20. Bowesfield (Tees Valley Wildlife Trust)
21. Portbury Wharf (Avon Wildlife Trust)
22. Ditchford Lakes and Meadows (The Wildlife Trust for Beds, Cambs and Northants)
23. Willington Gravel Pits (Derbyshire Wildlife Trust)
24. Red House (Montgomeryshire Wildlife Trust)
25. Doxey Marshes (Staffordshire Wildlife Trust)
26. Hockenhull Platts (Cheshire Wildlife Trust)
27. Ranworth Broad (Norfolk Wildlife Trust)
28. Barton Broad (Norfolk Wildlife Trust)
29. Shibdon Pond (Durham Wildlife Trust)
30. Nansmellyn Marsh (Corwall Wildlife Trust)
31. Wreay Woods (Cumbria Wildlife Trust)
32. Druridge Bay nature reserves (Northumberland Wildlife Trust)
33. Lower Moor Farm (Wiltshire Wildlife Trust)
34. Langford Lakes (Wiltshire Wildlife Trust)

With no fixed home, otters are generally unseen in the landscape, but leave behind visual clues. Keep your eyes peeled for five-toed webbed footprints on the riverbank, partly eaten fish, and spraints with a pleasant aroma. Seriously, otter droppings have a delightful smell. Some compare it to jasmine tea, others to violet. Freshly cut hay with a dash of fish works for me. So give it a sniff. If it is tapered and decidedly rancid, apologies, that was from a mink. Otter spraints reveal what the animal has been eating – fish bones, fur and feathers bound in dark tarry mucous. If it is slimy it is fresh.

When you do find positive signs, the next step is to

go to ground and get comfortable; the elusive mustelid may well be in the area. Focus your eyes on the water and banks; remain silent and still; watch and wait. There is no guarantee you will see an otter, but this makes any encounter all the more special. If the animal is present, the likelihood is that you have been seen – or rather smelt – first. Be patient. If an otter swims away beneath the safety of the water, a chain of bubbles will float to the surface, released from its fur. But then, bubbles could be from fish and the closest otter may well be miles away.

Cameraman and presenter Charlie Hamilton James introduced his young sons to otter spotting while filming *Halcyon River Diaries*. He said of the experience:

> My job, despite its romantic appeal, is for the most part very boring. It involves hours and hours of sitting doing absolutely nothing – something kids are bad at. It is not even patience, as people always suggest to me; it is the management of boredom, hunger, cold and needing a wee – all things that kids are also very bad at.

Those who lack patience should venture to Shetland, the best place to see wild otters in Europe. These creatures of habit live and feed in the sea, but use pathways known as otter highways to venture to freshwater inland. These grassy routes are regularly frequented and have a distinctive used appearance. Here, the otters can also be seen during the day. With all of this in mind, good luck, and happy otter spotting!

> Shetland is the best place to see otters in Britain.
> It seems to have just the right mix of good habitat
> and plentiful fish supplies... When I go out filming
> otters the first thing I do is look at the wind
> direction ... The trick when looking for otters is to
> be in a location where the wind is blowing either
> into your face as you travel along the beach or
> from the sea directly onto the land. If you get this
> wrong the chances of seeing otters are almost zero.
>
> —Charlie Hamilton James on
> the BBC's Nature UK blog, 2010

PLATYPUS

The patchwork appearance of the platypus (*Ornithorhynchus anatinus*) is truly unique. With a bill like a duck, eyes and body like a mole, webbed feet like an otter, tail like a beaver, and reptilian gait, it is not surprising that 18th-century zoologists thought early specimens were the creation of Chinese taxidermists. When George Shaw produced the first description of the Australian animal in 1799 he struggled to accept it was not a hoax, admitting, 'I almost doubt the testimony of my own eyes with respect to the structure of the animal's beak.' Imagine the confusion when it was discovered they are also egg-laying mammals (monotremes), and males can administer venom from a spur on their hind legs.

The platypus continues to amaze scientists. It has long been known that these animals close their eyes, ears and nose while underwater. In the 1980s, research found

receptors in their bill which indicated the presence of an added sense: electroreception. The use of electrical impulses to locate objects was previously only found in fish and amphibians. In 2008, a team of researchers led by Professor Chris Ponting unravelled the secrets of platypus DNA, revealing a genetic affinity with reptiles and birds. According to Ponting this represented 'the missing link in our understanding of how we and other mammals first evolved'. The platypus remains a zoological curiosity and genetic enigma. It also confirms the observation of French naturalist Buffon (1707–1788) that 'whatever was possible for Nature to produce has actually been produced'.

Platypus are not the only monotremes. They are joined by echidnas, named after the serpent-nymph from Greek mythology. Affectionately known as spiny ant eaters, the Western long-beaked echidna (*Zaglossus bruijni*), Sir David's long-beaked echidna (*Zaglossus attenboroughi*), and Eastern long-beaked echidna (*Zaglossus bartoni*) are endemic to Papua New Guinea. The short-beaked echidna (*Tachyglossus aculeatus*) is also found throughout Australia. Male echidnas also possess an evolutionary oddity, in the form of – wait for it – the four-headed penis!

CRACKED IT?

An age-old question has vexed the minds of our greatest thinkers: which came first, the chicken or the egg? The ancient world took the dilemma seriously. Greek philosopher Aristotle (384–322BC) could not imagine one without the other: 'If there has been a first man he must have been born without father or mother – which is repugnant to nature. For there could not have been a first egg to give a beginning to birds, or there should have been a first bird which gave a beginning to eggs; for a bird comes from an egg.'

Those from the Judeo-Christian tradition pointed to the Book of Genesis. If God created winged fowl, blessed them, and told them to be fruitful and multiply, then the chicken came before the egg. Roman historian Plutarch (AD46–126) recognised the broader significance of this seemingly trivial conundrum. In the Moralia he wrote that, in discussing this 'small problem ... we were rocking loose a great and heavy one, that of the creation of the world'.

Charles Darwin's theory of evolution took God out of the equation, proposing that species gradually change over time. For Darwin, eggs long pre-existed chickens. He maintained the domesticated species descended from the red jungle fowl (Gallus gallus), therefore an egg was laid, from which the first chicken was hatched. But then, if an egg from a non-chicken contained the first chicken, would that not make that egg the first chicken egg?

According to British scientists, this is not the case. Findings from a 2010 paper, 'Structural Control of Crystal Nuclei by an Eggshell Protein', suggested a protein called ovocledidin-17, or OC-17, is key. The first-named researcher Dr Colin Freeman, from Sheffield University, stated, 'It had long been suspected that the egg came first but now we have the scientific proof that shows that in fact the chicken came first.' As this protein is only found in chicken's ovaries, it is claimed that a chicken egg only exists if it has been created inside a chicken.

All of which means the score is, currently, 2–1 to the chicken. But then, to confuse matters further, Buddhists and other faiths that have a cyclical view of life would totally disagree, as they believe there was no creation, so there was no first ...

The case continues.

> 'A hen is only an egg's way of making another egg.'
> —Samuel Butler (1835–1902)

WHAT'S IN A NAME?

Latin may well be considered a dead language, but *binomial* names hold valuable clues about the physical characteristics and habitats of certain species. Fellow monoglots, there's no need to worry: lessons will not be required. Dixe Wills offers some sage advice in *The Armchair Naturalist* (2007). Remember these words and you're sure to become a better naturalist without really trying.

Appearance

cristat– = something with a crest
Crested Lark (*Galerida cristata*)
Great Crested Grebe (*Podiceps cristatus*)
Great Crested Newt (*Triturus cristatus*)

hirsut– = something hirsute (hairy)
Great Willowherb (*Epilobium hirsutum*)
Hairy Bitter-cress (*Cardamine hirsuta*)

minutus = something minute
Harvest Mouse (*Micromys minutus*)
Little Bittern (*Ixobrychus minutus*)
Sand Goby (*Pomatoschistus minutus*)

pseudo– = something that could be mistaken for something else
Douglas Fir (*Pseudotsuga menziesii*)
Sycamore (*Acer pseudoplatanus*)

ruf– = something reddish
Red-legged Partridge (*Alectoris rufa*)
European Red Slug (*Arion rufus*)

Habitat

aquatica = found in or near water
Reed Sweet Grass (*Glyceria aquatica*)
Water Spider (*Argyroneta aquatica*)

arborea = found in or resembling a tree
Tree Mallow (*Lavatera arborea*)
Woodlark (*Lullula arborea*)

arvens– = found in a field
Basil Thyme (*Acinos arvensis*)
Charlock (*Sinapis arvensis*)
Field Mouse-ear (*Cerastium arvense*)
Skylark (*Alauda arvensis*)

campestr– = found in a field
Field Maple (*Acer campestre*)
Field Mushroom (*Agaricus campestris*)
Green Tiger Beetle (*Cinindela campestris*)

pratens– = found in a meadow
Goatsbeard (*Tragopogon pratensis*)
Meadow Cranesbill (*Geranium pratense*)
Meadow Pipit (*Anthus pratensis*)

sylv– = found in a wood
Scots Pine (*Pinus sylvestris*)
Wood Mouse (*Apodemus sylvaticus*)

NAMING TROPICAL STORMS

'A storm lived and grew; no two were ever the same. He must name the baby. He considered a moment for more names in –ia, and thought of Maria. It was more homely than Antonia or Cornelia; it did not even sound like them. But it was a name ... Good luck Maria!'

—George Rippey Stewart, *Storm* (1941)

When hurricanes from the North Atlantic Ocean, cyclones from the Indian Ocean, and typhoons from the Pacific Ocean strike, they devastate everything in their path. Certain names then become forever associated with death and destruction. The naming process is not random, but has changed with time. In the 19th century, many hurricanes in the West Indies were named after the nearest saint's day. The devastating Hurricane Santa Ana, for instance, struck Puerto Rico on 26 July 1825. Landfall locations (where the storm first moves over land) have also been used such as for Galveston Hurricane of 1900, as have latitude-longitude identifications.

Australian meteorologist Clement Wragge (1852–1922), known as Wet Wragge to his friends, was the pioneer of naming storms. He used characters from mythology, letters of the Greek alphabet and names of people he did not like. Later, he chose only female names. George R. Stewart's 1941 novel *Storm* popularised this practice. The US National Hurricane Center started to officially name storms in 1951, using the old phonetic alphabet (Able, Baker, Charlie, etc.). From 1953 a new list of female names was adopted, to which male names were added from 1979.

Today the World Meteorological Organisation (WMO) is responsible for naming individual tropical storms. There are separate options for the Atlantic, Eastern North Pacific and Central North Pacific. The first two have six alphabetic lists which are used in rotation and recycled every six years. The latter is made up of four lists.

Some of the names below, earmarked for the Atlantic, will be hitting the headlines in the future. Will you have the misfortune of having a hurricane named after you?

2013	2014	2015	2016	2017	2018
Andrea	Arthur	Ana	Alex	Arlene	Alberto
Barry	Bertha	Bill	Bonnie	Bret	Beryl
Chantal	Cristobal	Claudette	Colin	Cindy	Chris
Dorian	Dolly	Danny	Danielle	Don	Debby
Erin	Edouard	Erika	Earl	Emily	Ernesto
Fernand	Fay	Fred	Fiona	Franklin	Florence
Gabrielle	Gonzalo	Grace	Gaston	Gert	Gordon
Humberto	Hanna	Henri	Hermine	Harvey	Helene
Ingrid	Isaias	Ida	Ian	Irma	Isaac
Jerry	Josephine	Joaquin	Julia	Jose	Joyce
Karen	Kyle	Kate	Karl	Katia	Kirk
Lorenzo	Laura	Larry	Lisa	Lee	Leslie
Melissa	Marco	Mindy	Matthew	Maria	Michael
Nestor	Nana	Nicholas	Nicole	Nate	Nadine
Olga	Omar	Odette	Otto	Ophelia	Oscar
Pablo	Paulette	Peter	Paula	Philippe	Patty
Rebekah	Rene	Rose	Richard	Rina	Rafael
Sebastien	Sally	Sam	Shary	Sean	Sandy*
Tanya	Teddy	Teresa	Tobias	Tammy	Tony
Van	Vicky	Victor	Virginie	Vince	Valerie
Wendy	Wilfred	Wanda	Walter	Whitney	William

* see overleaf regarding 'Sandy'

You probably spotted some famous omissions. There is no mention of Katrina (2005, US$108 billion damage), Ike (2008, $37.6bn), Wilma (2005, $29.2bn), Andrew (1992, $26.5bn), Agnes (1972, $15.2bn), Gilbert (1988, $10.2bn), Betsy (1965, $9.9bn), or Mitch (1998, $8.2bn). The reason for this is simple. The WMO decided it would be insensitive and confusing to reuse the names of the most destructive hurricanes. They are retired and replaced. Seventy-six names were retired between 1954 and 2011.

Sandy, which turned into a super storm in late October 2012, was the second costliest hurricane in US history ($75bn damage). Shortly before this book went to press, a public affairs officer with the National Hurricane Center stated, 'It is highly expected that the name "Sandy" will be retired.'

> 2005 was the most active Atlantic hurricane season on record. It reportedly caused $159.2 billion worth of damage, killed 3,913 and five names were retired: Dennis, Katrina, Rita, Stan and Wilma.

CONSERVATION MOVEMENT

Bill Adams, Professor of Conservation and Development at the University of Cambridge, maintains that 'Conservation is never anything but social and never anything but political.' The conservation movement should be seen as a collection of causes, each with its own social values, agendas and histories. Paul Jepson and Richard Ladle, co-authors of *Conservation. A Beginner's Guide* (2010), note that as well as protecting species and places, conservationists govern our relationship with the natural world. The origin and associated values of such campaigns are described here:

Wise-use movement
British colonies, 18th century; Unites States, early 20th century
Scientists advised governments that healthy ecosystems are essential for safeguarding economic growth, social stability and quality livelihoods. Natural resources were managed for the greatest good for the greatest number for the longest time.

Wilderness movement
California, late 19th century
Artists, philosophers and writers called for the preservation of wilderness – wild landscapes appreciated for their aesthetic, spiritual and physical benefits. These places were also seen as a benchmark to assess urban-industrial modernity.

Wildlife movement
New York, late 19th century; London, early 20th century
Big-game hunters, entrepreneurs and politicians recognised that wanton slaughter threatened species survival. A moral responsibility was accepted to prevent wiping out vulnerable wildlife.

Open-spaces movement

London, mid-19th century; New York, early 20th century
Social reformers and urban planners argued that urban residents required free access to nature for their health and well-being.

Nature monument movement

Western European cities, early 20th century
Natural historians and other prominent figures assert that an aesthetic and intellectual understanding of nature is central to the biological and cultural inheritance of many peoples. Monuments of nature should be protected.

> 'I do not see "people" and "nature" as opposed. Indeed, I do not believe that they are ultimately separable. Can people live with nature? Of course: there is no question about that. We can do nothing else – live or die, we are part of nature.'
>
> —Bill Adams, *Against Extinction: The Story of Conservation* (2004)

ENDANGERED

The term 'endangered' is regularly bandied around for different species, but the broader definition is not commonly known. The International Union for the Conservation of Nature define a species as endangered if one or more of the following criteria are met:

1. Very significant reduction in population size (70 per cent reduction over a ten-year or three-generation period)
2. Very significant reduction in geographic areas (restricted to less than 5,000km^2)
3. Population size estimated to be fewer than 2,500 (evidence of rapid decline of mature individuals)
4. Population size estimated to be fewer than 250 mature individuals
5. Probability of extinction in the wild is at least 20 per cent (within twenty years or five generations)

KAKAPO

'The kakapo is a bird out of time,' Douglas Adams (1952–2001) wrote in *Last Chance to See* (1990). 'If you look one in its large, round, greeny-brown face, it has a look of serenely innocent incomprehension that makes you want to hug it and tell it that everything will be all right, though you know that it probably will not be.' The strange appearance and peculiar ways of the world's rarest parrot certainly endears it to those who encounter it. Andrew Macalister of the Kakapo Recovery Programme admits, 'It is a Dr Seuss kind of bird – a parrot that can't fly, a nocturnal herbivore of the forest floor, a feathered heavyweight that can hop like a sparrow and growl like a dog.'

In 2009 the BBC broadcast *Last Chance to See*, a television series which saw Mark Carwardine revisiting the endangered species he researched 20 years previously with Douglas Adams. On this occasion, his travel companion was Stephen Fry. The critically endangered kakapo (*Strigops habroptilus*) of New Zealand had seen its population rise from just 40 birds to 124.

The series is probably best remembered for one rather unexpected, albeit comical moment when a kakapo called Sirocco climbed onto Carwardine's shoulders and attempted to mate with the back of his head. The parrot rose to international fame through social media, raising global awareness for the previously overlooked species, and much-needed funds to help protect them. New Zealand Prime Minister John Key even appointed Sirocco as Official Spokesbird for Conservation in 2010. 'He's a very media-savvy bird, he's got a worldwide fan base – they hang on every squawk that comes out of his beak. He'll be a great official spokesbird and a great ambassador for New Zealand.' A Department of Conservation spokesperson was thrilled by the worldwide attention:

> You can't buy the publicity that has come out of Sirocco's amorous attentions ... New Zealand has a lot of birds – it doesn't have elephants, lions, tigers or bears – we have something that people around the world think is fascinating and worth protecting.

As one of the world's most influential conservationists, this is the sort of immediate global impact Carwardine has always worked towards. It would be rather unfortunate if after decades of research he was to be remembered as the man, as Stephen Fry so eloquently phrased it, whose head was 'shagged by a rare parrot'.

> 'If naturalists go to heaven (about which there is considerable ecclesiastical doubt), I hope that I will be furnished with a troop of kakapo to amuse me in the evening instead of television.'
>
> —Gerald Durrell (1925–1995)

BIODIVERSITY HOTSPOTS

Biodiversity hotspots are areas with exceptional concentrations of endemic species (found nowhere else on Earth) that are undergoing significant habitat loss. The British ecologist Norman Myers first identified ten tropical forest hotspots in 1988. His concept was adopted by Conservation International the following year, which saw the number of identified hotspots rise to eighteen in 1990, 25 in 1996, 34 in 2005, and 35 in 2011. To qualify, a region must:

- Contain at least 1,500 species of vascular plants (0.5 per cent of the world's total) as endemics.
- Have lost at least 70 per cent of its original habitat.

More and more natural environments are disappearing in front of our very eyes, threatening over 50 per cent of the world's plant species and 42 per cent of all terrestrial vertebrate species. The 35 biodiversity hotspots in most desperate need of protection are:

Africa (8)
- Cape Floristic Region

- Coastal Forests of Eastern Africa
- Eastern Afromontane
- Guinean Forests of West Africa
- Horn of Africa
- Madagascar and the Indian Ocean Islands
- Maputaland-Pondoland-Albany
- Succulent Karoo

Europe and Central Asia (4)
- Caucasus
- Irano-Anatolian
- Mediterranean Basin
- Mountains of Central Asia

East Asia (2)
- Japan
- Mountains of Southwest China

South Asia (3)
- Himalaya, India
- Indo-Burma, India and Myanmar
- Western Ghats, India

South East Asia and Asia-Pacific (9)
- East Melanesian Islands
- Forests of East Australia
- New Caledonia
- New Zealand
- Philippines
- Polynesia-Micronesia

- Southwest Australia
- Sundaland
- Wallacea

North and Central America (4)
- California Floristic Province
- Caribbean Islands
- Madrean pine-oak woodlands
- Mesoamerica

South America (5)
- Atlantic Forest
- Cerrado
- Chilean Winter Rainfall and Valdivian Forests
- Tumbes-Chocó-Magdalena
- Tropical Andes

The nation thought to have the highest rate of biodiversity in the world is Brazil, representing an impressive 20 per cent of all life on the planet. Within the 8.5 million km^2 territory an estimated 103,870 animal species and up to 49,000 plant species are found. According to the Brazilian Ministry of the Environment, and National Center of Flora Conservation, only 7,302 animal and 40,000 plant species have been scientifically described. Boasting six biomes, two of which have biodiversity hotspot status (Mata Atlântica and Cerrado), and 700 animals 'discovered' every year, Brazil is an exciting place for species seekers and adventurous naturalists to explore.

MOST POLLUTED

In 2010, an infographic published in *Power & Energy* magazine, based on findings by the Blacksmith Institute, revealed that the world's top ten most polluted places were:

1. **Sumgayit, Azerbaijan.** Home to 40 chemical factories. Cancer rates here are 50 per cent above average.

2. **Linfen, China.** This major coal-mining area has the worst air quality in China.

3. **Tianying, China.** China's foremost lead-producing area. Lead concentrations here are ten times the national standard.

4. **Sukinda, India.** A centre for chromite ore mining. The drinking water contains high levels of hexavalent chromium.

5. **Vapi, India.** A sprawling industrial area. Mercury levels in groundwater are 96 times higher than WHO standards.

6. **La Oroya, Peru.** A polymetallic smelter affects the blood–lead levels and life expectancy of the 35,000 population.

7. **Dzerzhinsk, Russia.** A chemical waste disposal site. Dioxin levels in the water are up to 17 million times the safe limit.

8. **Norilsk, Russia.** The world's largest heavy metal smelting complex releases 2 million tons of carbon dioxide annually.

9. **Chernobyl, Ukraine.** The location of the world's worst nuclear disaster in 1986. Infertility and birth defects are still high.

10. **Kabwe, Zambia.** A former zinc- and lead-mining area. Residents remain exposed to toxic levels of lead.

BIOSECURITY BRITAIN

Over the last decade or so, Britain's farming industry has been blighted by disease. In 2001 the countryside was closed for business due to a foot and mouth outbreak. The military formed blockades and assisted with the mass extermination of nearly 6.5 million livestock. The resulting biocide unfolded in front of our eyes – the burning pyres of carcasses shocked the world.

Avian influenza got the nation into a flutter in 2007, when an outbreak was discovered at the Bernard Matthews poultry farms in Suffolk. As a zoonotic disease (one that can pass between animals and humans) the nation was right to be concerned. Discovered on 30 January, a 3km protection zone, 10km surveillance zone and 2,000km^2 restricted zone were set up. 159,000 turkeys were slaughtered by 5 February. The disease did not spread.

In 2013, bovine tuberculosis is in the news. Seventy per cent of badgers in selected cull zones will be killed in an attempt to reduce the spread of infection in cattle. This has led to an impassioned campaign to save the badgers, led by animal welfarist and former Queen guitarist Brian May, who maintains that 'vaccination is the only long-term cure'.

Strategies for disease monitoring and prevention often go unnoticed, as do the diseases that are kept at bay. Those of most concern to the British government's Department of Environment, Food and Rural Affairs (DEFRA) are listed as 'notifiable' diseases. If suspected, animal keepers are legally required to report any signs to the Animal Health Veterinary Laboratories Agency (AHVLA). The following list will make you more aware of the finer details about causes and symptoms.

Notifiable diseases

African horse sickness (AHS)
A highly infectious insect-borne disease, which can prove fatal for horses, mules and donkeys.

Avian influenza (AI, bird flu)
A highly contagious viral disease affecting many species of birds.

Bovine spongiform encephalopathy (BSE)
More commonly known as 'mad cow disease', a fatal neurodegenerative disease in cattle that causes a spongy degeneration in the brain and spinal cord.

Bovine tuberculosis (TB)
The bacterium *Mycobacterium bovis* (M. bovis) infects and causes TB in cattle, badgers, deer, goats, pigs, camelids, dogs and cats, and most other mammals.

Bluetongue (BTV)
Bluetongue is an exotic disease affecting all ruminants – mammals that chew the cud regurgitated from its rumen. This includes sheep, cattle, deer, goats and camelids.

Contagious equine metritis (CEM)
A venereal bacterial disease that affects horses.

Equine infectious anaemia (EIA, swamp fever)
An exotic viral disease that affects horses, mules and donkeys.

Equine viral arteritis (EVA)
An acute, contagious, viral disease in horses caused by the equine arteritis virus (EAV).

European bat lyssavirus (EBLV)
This fatal viral disease is more commonly known as bat rabies or rabies in bats. It can affect all mammals, including humans, if no treatment is received.

Foot-and-mouth disease (FMD)
An infectious disease largely affecting cloven-hoofed animals.

Newcastle disease
A highly contagious disease of birds caused by a paramyxo virus.

Rabies (classical)
All mammals are potentially susceptible to this fatal disease, if no treatment is received.

> 'Biosecurity, as a response to threats from zoonotic, food-borne and emerging infectious diseases, implies and is often understood in terms of a spatial segregation of forms of life, a struggle to separate healthy life from diseased bodies.'
> —Steve Hinchliffe, 'Biosecurity and the topologies of infected life', *Transactions of the Institute of British Geographers* (2012)

TB OR NOT TB

The bovine tuberculosis and badger cull debate revolves around numbers. Of course there are political, economic and moral aspects which regularly make the news but it is the uncertain science, the seemingly insignificant benefits of killing native wildlife, which makes people so emotional about the subject. Here are some of the figures which have caused so much debate:

- £500 million spent on tackling bovine TB in the past ten years, at the expense of the UK taxpayer

- 5.5 million: total number of TB tests on cattle in England in 2011

- 26,000: approximate number of cattle slaughtered for TB control in England in 2011

- 35,000 cattle slaughtered after developing TB in 2012

- £150 million compensation for farmers and other costs

- £1 billion: estimated cost over next ten years if no direct action is taken

- 300,000: estimated badger population

- 150,000+ people signed a petition against the cull in 2012

- Four-year scheme of annual culling to be piloted, starting in 2013

- Six: number of weeks annual culls will last for

- 70 per cent of badgers to be killed in selected cull zones

- 5,000: projected number of badgers to be culled each year

- Anticipated 16 per cent reduction in the number of cattle herds affected by TB over a nine year period

- £2,500: average cost of culling by cage-trapping per km^2

- £300: average cost of shooting free-ranging badgers per km^2

- £1,000: average cost for a mixture of trapping and shooting per km^2

- £43.7 million invested by DEFRA in cattle and badger vaccination since 1997

- £15.5 million planned investment in further vaccine development over the next four years

- £2,250: average cost of vaccinating badgers with injectable badger vaccine (badger BCG) per km^2 per year

The bovine TB badger debate is not a simple case of 'to cull or not to cull'. Individuals from the farming community, politicians, conservationists, animal welfarists and animal rights advocates have their own approaches and intentions. For one moment, clear the rhetoric from your mind, look at the information above and make a judgement. What would you do?

ROADKILL

'Have you ever eaten otter?'

'I'm afraid not.'

'I have. I've got some badger pie in the freezer if you want to come over for lunch tomorrow.'

Arthur Boyt has gained a reputation as the roadkill connoisseur of Cornwall. Although I did not accept his kind offer of lunch on that occasion, the encounter made me fascinated by the subject.

The ethics of meat eating has become increasingly tied to an animal's experience of life and mode of death. It is the perceived edibility of an embodied carcass which sanctions its role as meat. Roadkill-as-food is considered by some as ethical and organic meat, without the moral dilemma of intentional killing. Despite this, the majority of the public seem disgusted at the thought.

In terms of availability, there is no shortage of roadkill. According to the People's Trust for Endangered Species (PTES) about a million mammals die on Britain's roads each year, plus 3 million pheasants and 7 million other birds. Across the Atlantic cars are also a massive killer. The Humane Society of the United States estimates that a million animals are killed by vehicles every day.

Those who eat roadkill are often frowned upon, even mocked. But then, it is free, it is fresh, and it is natural. Unlike the meat industry, the source is identifiable and you know exactly what you are eating. Another roadkill diner, Alison Brierley, said:

When I see a tray of pre-packaged meat I often wonder how the animal had been fed, looked after, respected and finally slaughtered. Did the animal suffer? What has been pumped into it? Is it full of antibiotics and growth hormones? What food had it been eating? Do I want this piece of meat in my body?

Since the horsemeat scandal of 2013, when British and Irish consumers were subjected to a series of revelations about the presence of horsemeat in various 'beef' products, these questions are more relevant than ever before. This alternative form of meat-eating challenges us to reassess our relationship with the natural world. People for the Ethical Treatment of Animals (PETA), for example, reluctantly support the practice: 'If people must eat animal carcasses, roadkill is a superior option to the neatly shrink-wrapped plastic packages of meat in the supermarket.'

As somebody who struggles with their carnivorous guilty conscience, roadkill is a food I will graciously accept in the future.

'I have eaten rabbit, blue hare, brown hare, pheasant, partridge, fallow deer, roe deer, muntjac, badger, otter, fox, vole, horseshoe bat, long-eared bat, barn owl, porcupine, possum, gallinule, kea, wallaby, wood pigeon, racing pigeon, feral pigeon, collared dove, rook, swan, duck, moorhen, grouse, blackbird, Canada goose, cat, dog, stoat, grass snake, sheep, and possibly others.'

—Arthur Boyt

BAITING, FIGHTING, HUNTING

The term 'blood sports' was first adopted by the Humanitarian League in the 1890s to condemn sports in which 'pleasure was obtained at the cost of suffering to animals'. Such sports have been widely supported in the British Isles, from now-prohibited practices such as animal baiting, fighting and coursing to the hunting and shooting rituals that – despite opposition – remain popular today.

In recent years perceptions of cruelty have clouded the reasons why people have enjoyed killing animals for sport. Those reasons are various and complex, but central factors include the unique sporting identity of each activity, and its associated code of conduct. The respective sportsmen required various degrees of skill, stamina and strength, as well as an intimate knowledge of the animals involved and their environments.

Bear-baiting and bull-baiting, in which the baited animal would be tethered to the ground and then made to fight for its life against one or more dogs, first became popular in England during the reign of Henry II (1154–1189). The bears and bulls were appreciated for their size, strength and tenacity, the smaller dogs respected for their ingenuity, ferocity and fighting spirit. It was claimed that the effect of such contests on the spectator was to 'inspire courage, produce a nobleness of sentiment, and, elevation of mind.'

The notion of perceived 'fairness' was also central to both cockfighting and dog-fighting. In these spectacles, evenly matched animals would fight to the death in specially built pits. An Act of Parliament was passed in 1835 outlawing animal baiting and fighting. However, bull-baiting continued long into the 19th century, and the baiting of badgers is still illegally practiced in clandestine locations today – as are cockfighting and dog-fighting.

In the British countryside, sports revolving around the hunting of solitary animals with hounds have traditionally enjoyed great popularity. Prized quarries have included the wolf, the boar, the hare, the rabbit, the fox, the otter and the 'king of all venery', the deer. The subsequent rise of the fox as a valued sporting adversary was the consequence of a widespread clearing of woodlands and an accompanying reduction of deer. New hound-breeding techniques were developed in the 1750s by Hugo Meynell, earning him the epithet 'father of modern fox-hunting', and as a result foxhounds came to enjoy improved speed, stamina and scenting ability. With these developments, the exhilaration of the chase heightened, and the demands for horsemanship increased. The huntsman also required a broader range of skills, which were defined by writer and huntsman Peter Beckford (1740–1811) as 'a clear head, nice apprehension, undaunted courage, strength of constitution, activity of body, a good ear, and a good voice.'

Hunting with hounds was banned in Britain under the Hunting with Dogs Act of 2004. Yet modern forms of fox-hunting, whereby hounds follow an artificial scent, continue to enjoy strong support. In 2012, the traditional annual highlight of the Boxing Day meet saw 250,000 people turn out to enjoy their local hunt. Despite opposition, the hunting community is optimistic about the future of its sport – the current Conservative-led coalition government has proposed a free vote to repeal the ban.

* Based on a longer piece by Daniel Allen entitled 'Animal Blood Sports, British Isles', published in Nauright & Parrish (eds) *Sports Around the World* (ABC-CLIO, 2012)

> 'The English country gentleman galloping after a fox
> – the unspeakable in full pursuit of the uneatable.'
> —Oscar Wilde (1854–1900)

THE VOYAGE OF H.M.S. BEAGLE

Charles Darwin notched up a fine collection of first-time experiences on the five-year voyage on H.M.S. *Beagle*. On returning to England on 2 October 1836, Darwin's memories included the 'intense delight' of seeing his first tropical forest, being 'wonderfully lucky with fossil bones' and 'primitive looking rocks', discovering unique birds, animals and plants on the Galapagos Islands, and marvelling at marsupials and coral reefs in Australia.

A DAY AT LONDON ZOO
WITH CHARLES DARWIN

The collection and display of exotic animals can be traced back to ancient Egypt. An archaeological excavation in 2009 found evidence that the earliest known menagerie existed in 3500BC. The Hierakonpolis Expedition revealed

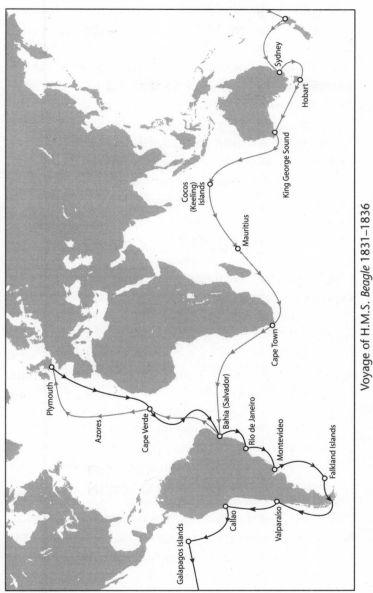

Voyage of H.M.S. *Beagle* 1831–1836

animal burials in an elite cemetery, suggesting the ancient Egyptian rulers kept exotics in captivity. Among the 112 remains were eleven baboons, six wildcats, three hippos and two elephants. The world's first scientific zoo was founded by the Zoological Society of London in 1828. Initially a private collection, members visited to study the living specimens with the aim of advancing zoology and animal physiology. When the gates opened to the public in 1847, crowds flocked to see the curiosities on display.

Jenny the Orang-utan was the new sensation at London Zoo in 1837. Having never seen an ape before, Charles Darwin visited the zoo on 28 March 1838. He climbed into the enclosure with Jenny and spent hours observing her. The encounter made a lasting impression, especially her childlike emotions and movements. Darwin wrote in his notebook:

> Let man visit Ouranoutang in domestication, hear its expressive whine, see its intelligence when spoken to; as if it understands every word said ... see its passion & rage, sulkiness, & very actions of despair; ... and then let him boast of his proud pre-eminence ... Man in his arrogance thinks himself a great work, worthy the interposition of a deity. More humble and I believe true to consider him created from animals.

Two decades before the publication of *On the Origin of Species by Means of Natural Selection* (1859), and three before *The Descent of Man, and Selection in Relation to Sex* (1871), Darwin was privately writing about the common ancestry of humans and apes.

When Queen Victoria met the replacement orang-
utan, also named Jenny, in 1842, she described her as
'too wonderful' but also 'frightfully, and painfully, and
disagreeably human'. Queen Victoria was fascinated by
the creature, but repulsed by her human-like qualities.
If the opinion of the monarch can be taken to be representative of at least a section of the population, Darwin's
decision to keep his world-changing thoughts to himself, is put into perspective.

THE HIPPOPOTAMUS POLKA

On 25 May 1850 a young hippopotamus called Obaysch
arrived by ship in Southampton, then travelled by train
to London Zoo. Touted as the first living hippo to set
foot in Europe since the Roman Empire, his arrival stim-
ulated a nationwide craze, that the newspapers termed
'hippomania'. At London Zoo he was instantly the star
attraction. Crowds gathered at the hippo house to see
the mysterious creature. Memorabilia was sold. His presence doubled the zoo's annual attendance figures from
168,895 in 1849 to 360,402 in 1850.

Obaysch even inspired a popular song by Louis
St Mars, 'The Hippopotamus Polka' (1850). According to
a letter that accompanied the sheet music, from a Lady
Mary, the idea came from an encounter she had shared
with two friends while watching the lumbering exhibit:

> ... you know Emily's love of sarcasm, and her pen-
> chant for uttering witticisms – while gazing at

the gambols of the animal in the water, she slyly remarked to me 'how graceful; he reminds me strongly of Lord A—— the other evening when dancing the polka when dancing with Lady Jane ——d.' We were much amused at the comparison … I mentioned the matter to ——, whose musical invention you much admire.

Front cover of the sheet music for 'The Hippopotamus Polka'

With this original composition, the clumsiness of the hippo and wit of polite Victorian society could be expressed through music and dance. Obaysch was an instant favourite with the satiric press. *Punch* magazine regularly published articles referring to the life of the hippopotamus in a strange land. One titled 'Hip, Hip, Hip, for the Hippopotamus' read:

> EVERYBODY is still running towards the Regent's Park, for the purpose of passing half an hour with the Hippopotamus. The animal itself repays public curiosity with a yawn of indifference, or throws cold water on the ardour of his visitors, by suddenly plunging into his bath, and splashing everyone within five yards of him.
>
> Much disappointment has been expressed at the Hippopotamus, in consequence of its not being exactly up to the general idea of a sea-horse, and many hundreds go away grumbling every day, because the brute is not so equestrian in appearance as could be desired.

Aside from mocking the observers for their faddish and uncultured ways, *Punch* was right: Obaysch did not do much.

After a year of excitement and enthusiasm, hippomania started to fade. Obaysch was a sensational curiosity, but his characteristics were not as entertaining as those of other animals on display. New acquisitions, such as an elephant calf in 1851, took the shine off the hippo.

Obaysch went on to spend another 27 years in the zoo. No doubt he lazily observed the arrival of the next sensation, Jumbo in 1865; and yawned as he became the most famous elephant in the world. Obaysch died on 11 March 1878.

JUMBO MANIA

A hundred thousand children wrote heartfelt letters to Queen Victoria pleading her to intervene in the sale of Jumbo (1861–1885). It made little difference. P.T. Barnum (1810–1891) had already paid London Zoo $10,000 for the world's largest elephant and was making arrangements to ship him to New York. After seventeen years of being the much-loved 'pet of the zoo', 1881 was the year Jumbo mania headed to the United States.

A fond but bitter farewell in the *London Daily Telegraph* reflected the country's mood:

> No more quiet garden strolls, no shady trees, green lawns, and flowery thickets ... Our amiable monster must dwell in a tent, take part in the routine of a circus, and, instead of his by-gone friendly trots with British girls and boys, and perpetual luncheons on buns and oranges, must amuse a Yankee mob, and put up with peanuts and waffles.

Jumbo's 'wife' Alice was also heartbroken. 'Jumbo's gone and left me; What am I to do? He's gone across the briny sea/To Barnum's Yankee Zoo' read a memorial card from the Zoological Gardens. Across the Atlantic, Jumbo became the star attraction in 'The Greatest Show on Earth', and the most famous elephant in the world. During his four years in the circus, 16 million adults and 4 million children paid to see him walking around the tent.

On 15 September 1885 Jumbo was tragically killed by an unscheduled freight train but even this untimely death did not diminish his fame. Barnum arranged for the hide to be stuffed and the skeleton to be displayed and these remains toured with the circus from 1886, as did the 'widowed' Alice, acquired from London Zoo. 'Jumbo Stuffed a Greater Attraction than Jumbo Alive,' reported the *New York Times*.

After a short return to England with the circus in the winter of 1889, the hide returned to America and was retired at Tufts University, Massachusetts. The skin of Jumbo was proudly displayed until 16 April 1975, when Barnum Hall was destroyed by a fire.

SOFT GOLD

In 1741 Vitus Bering set off on an expedition to map the west coast of Alaska. When the storm-ravaged ship ran ashore and the captain died, the remaining crew made shelters and survived by eating sea cows, seals and sea otters. They found the sea otter particularly easy to kill. Among the bored men, gambling was prevalent, and otter skins became the main prize. The qualities of this fur did not go unnoticed by Georg Wilhelm Steller

(1709–1746), the appointed naturalist of the expedition. He wrote, 'These animals are very beautiful, and because of their beauty are very valuable, as one may well believe of a skin the hairs of which, an inch or an inch and a half in length, are very soft, very thickly set, jet black and glossy.' Ranging from 26,000 to 165,000 hairs per square centimetre, the sea otter has the densest coat in the animal kingdom.

When the 46 surviving members constructed a new vessel in 1742, they eventually returned to Russia with nearly 700 pelts. Steller credited the sea otter for their survival, insisting the animal deserved 'great reverence' for preventing scurvy and starvation. The arrival of these new skins caused quite a sensation, especially in China, where the Manchu upper classes initially paid up to US$100 per pelt. As these high prices were unrivalled in the trade, the sea otter soon became known as 'soft gold'. The sea otter effectively belonged to the Russians until the 1780s, as they kept the commercial value of the animal a closely guarded secret. When explorers and traders learnt that sea otters were essentially floating fortunes, there was a frenzied rush to the northwest Pacific coast. Hundreds of ships were sent from Britain, Spain, France and America, and the sought-after fur reached the heights of fashion in St Petersburg, Paris, London and Boston. An estimated 750,000 or more skins were sold by everyone involved between 1745 and 1822.

In 1867, the United States purchased Alaska from the Russian Empire for $7,200,000. An American firm also bought the rights to the Russian-American Company that year, renaming it the Alaska Commercial Company.

Over the next 40 years fur traders reaped the rewards, with profits from skin sales far exceeding the price paid for the Alaskan territory. This unregulated exploitation was exterminating the species: the Alaska Commercial Company only found 31 animals in 1900. The sea otter was on the brink of extinction, with a population less than 2,000. The organised killing finally ended in 1911 when the United States, Russia, Great Britain and Japan agreed the Fur Seal Treaty. This was reinforced in California by federal law in 1913. Under these enactments the sea otter gained legal protection across the world for the first time in its history. Remarkably, in just 170 years almost 1 million animals were slaughtered for fashion. Perhaps not the 'great reverence' Georg Wilhelm Steller had in mind for the species which had saved the lives of him and his shipmates.

Extract from *Otter* by Daniel Allen (Reaktion Books, 2010)

A misconception in the British media is that sea otters live on the coasts of Scotland. They do not. Sea otters (*Enhydra lutris*) live in the Pacific. Those seen in Scotland are Eurasian otters (*Lutra lutra*) which happen to live beside the sea. 'Scottish coastal otters' is a far more accurate description.

TIGERTIME

When you look at an image of a wild tiger (*Panthera tigris*), what do you see? The largest cat in the world? Majestic beauty? The striking orange coat and distinctive black stripes? An endangered species? One of only 3,200 remaining individuals? A conservation icon? A powerful predator? A man-killer? A hunting trophy? A rug? A roaming medicine cabinet to be poached, cut up, and sold as traditional remedies? A future extinction?

At the beginning of the 20th century there were an estimated 40,000 wild tigers in India. Today there are just 1,400. In this time, three of the eight tiger subspecies around the world (Bali, Caspian and Javan) have also become extinct.

Habitat loss, human conflict and illegal poaching have put this species in crisis. Despite banning the trade of tiger parts in 1993, China remains the largest market. The growing middle classes happily pay for traditional remedies; farmers, smugglers and alternative medicine traders continue making large profits.

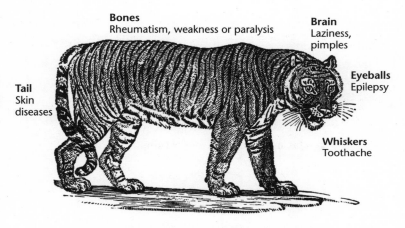

Bones
Rheumatism, weakness or paralysis

Brain
Laziness,
pimples

Eyeballs
Epilepsy

Tail
Skin
diseases

Whiskers
Toothache

How tiger parts are used in alternative medicine

Various tiger conservation charities are working to save the species. American actor Leonardo DiCaprio made a million-dollar commitment to the WWF campaign. 'If we don't take action now, one of the most iconic animals on our planet could be gone in just a few decades,' explained DiCaprio.

The David Shepherd Wildlife Foundation also launched TigerTime, a worldwide movement aimed at tackling poachers, raising awareness, funding conservation partners, lobbying governments and ultimately saving the tiger. Wildlife artist David Shepherd CBE makes this passionate plea for support: 'We can talk all day long about how to save the tiger – but the truth is simple; the killing has to stop! I'm not prepared to see tigers lost to the world and I want everyone who shares my view to stand with me and be heard.'

At the time of writing this entry, 205,405 people are standing beside David. This includes celebrity support from Sir Paul McCartney, Joanna Lumley OBE, Susan Sarandon, Jeremy Irons, Ricky Gervais and Stephen Fry. Your humble corvid guide has become number 205,406. Can you really imagine a world without wild tigers? Show your support with a signature; together we can save this species.

EARTH DAY

Reverence for life on our planet is such that one day is not enough to celebrate it. The United Nations (UN) recognises two annual events.

Earth Day was initially the idea of American peace activist John McConnell. At the March 1969 UNESCO conference he proposed having an international holiday 'to celebrate the wonder of life on our planet'. Recognising that a date was needed to draw people together, McConnell chose 21 March, the first day of the spring equinox in the northern hemisphere. In 1970 his Earth Day Proclamation was signed and celebrated in California; the next year it was sanctioned by the United Nations. U Thant, the UN Secretary-General, supported the global initiative, stating, 'May there be only peaceful and cheerful Earth Days to come for our beautiful Spaceship Earth as it continues to spin and circle in frigid space with its warm and fragile cargo of animate life.' The Earth Society Foundation has ensured that this Earth Day continues to be recognised as a global symbol, celebrating 'at the moment when the amount of light and the amount of darkness on Earth are equal' – the March equinox.

An unrelated incident, the Santa Barbara oil spill of January and February 1969, inspired US Senator Gaylord Nelson to organise an alternative Earth Day. Dismayed by the destruction from the then-largest oil spill in American waters, Nelson was determined to put the environment on the political agenda. The youth of the nation was central to this. 'I am convinced,' Nelson argued, 'that all we need to do to bring an overwhelming insistence of the new generation that we stem the tide of environmental disaster is to present the facts clearly and dramatically.' He proposed that every university in the United States should set aside one day for an environmental teach-in.

On 22 April 1970, 20 million Americans showed their support. This version of Earth Day has grown every year, and is recognised as a pivotal moment for the modern green movement. In 2009 the UN designated 22 April International Mother Earth Day. The 50 member states acknowledged that 'the Earth and its ecosystems are our home' and agreed that 'it is necessary to promote harmony with nature and the Earth'. Today more than 1 billion people from 192 countries observe this Earth Day.

> 'The wealth of a nation is its air, water, soil, forests, minerals, rivers, lakes, oceans, scenic beauty, wildlife habitats and biodiversity. That's the whole economy. These biological systems are the sustaining wealth of the world.'
> —Gaylord Nelson, 1995

EARTH ENERGY

The violence and sheer power of nature is hard to put into words. That is why scientists find diagrams so useful. The diagram opposite, based on one by geophysicists Seth Stein and Michael Wysession puts this into perspective, by showing the energy release of earthquakes compared with other natural and man-made explosions.

EARTHQUAKE FATALITIES

The Great Chilean Earthquake of 22 May 1960 is the most powerful on record, with a magnitude of 9.5. Having struck in the afternoon in a region where earthquake-resistant buildings had been constructed, the death toll was relatively low at 1,655. The five deadliest earthquakes of the 20th century may not have been as powerful, but their wrath accounted for a total of 783,000 human lives.

Date	Magnitude	Region	Fatalities
27/28 July 1976	7.8	China, Tangshan	242,800
16 December 1920	8.5	China, Gansu	235,000
1 September 1923	7.8	Japan, Tokyo	142,800
28 December 1908	7.2	Italy, Messina	85,900
25 December 1932	7.6	China, Kansu	77,000

The 2010 Haiti earthquake was the most catastrophic in the first decade of the 21st century, killing an estimated 316,000, injuring 300,000, and displacing 1.3 million. Striking the most populated region of the poorest country

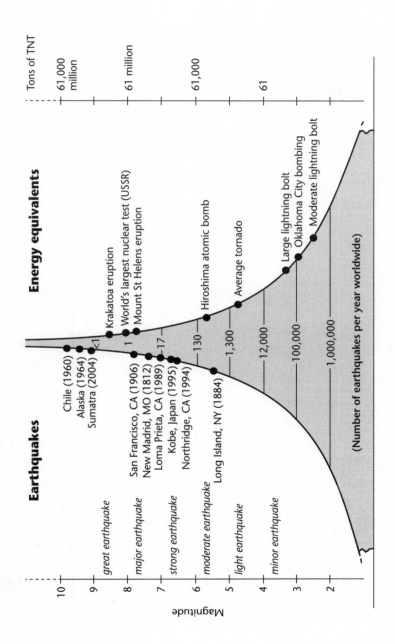

Earthquakes — Energy equivalents

Magnitude

Magnitude		
10		
9	great earthquake	Chile (1960) · Alaska (1964) · Sumatra (2004)
8	major earthquake	Krakatoa eruption · World's largest nuclear test (USSR) · Mount St Helens eruption · San Francisco, CA (1906) · New Madrid, MO (1812) · Loma Prieta, CA (1989)
7	strong earthquake	Kobe, Japan (1995) · Northridge, CA (1994)
6	moderate earthquake	Hiroshima atomic bomb · Long Island, NY (1884)
5	light earthquake	Average tornado
4	minor earthquake	Large lightning bolt · Oklahoma City bombing · Moderate lightning bolt
3		
2		

Tons of TNT: 61,000 million · 61 million · 61,000 · 61

(Number of earthquakes per year worldwide)
<1, 1, 17, 130, 1,300, 12,000, 100,000, 1,000,000

in the Western Hemisphere meant that Haitian residents had a low chance of survival. An estimated one in every fifteen people affected died. The five deadliest earthquakes for this decade alone accounted for 742,846 deaths.

Date	Magnitude	Region	Fatalities
12 January 2010	7.0	Haiti	316,000
26 December 2004	9.1	Off West Coast of Northern Sumatra	227,898
12 March 2008	7.9	Eastern Sichuan, China	87,587
8 October 2005	7.6	Pakistan	80,361
26 December 2003	6.6	Southeastern Iran	31,000

The deadliest earthquake ever recorded hit Shaanxi (Shensi), China on 23 January 1556. The tremor caused fissures, landslides, liquefaction, sandblows, subsidence, and uplift. City walls, civilian houses and temples were demolished. A staggering 830,000 lives were lost.

VOLCANIC ERUPTIONS

The six main types of volcano differ in their appearance and explosivity. This is largely down to the characteristics of magma. In high-viscosity magma, gas pressures build up, leading to violent eruptions. Thicker lava means that eruption columns hold their shape for longer, and the lower the silica content the faster the pyroclastic flow. In terms of explosivity the Plinian eruption is generally highest ranking, then Pelean, Vulcanian, Strombolian, Hawaiian, and Icelandic.

Plinian eruption

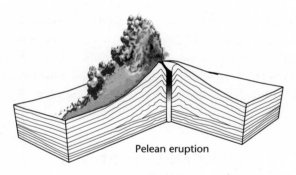

Pelean eruption

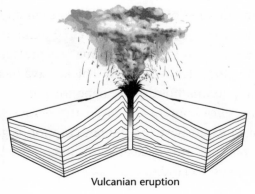

Vulcanian eruption

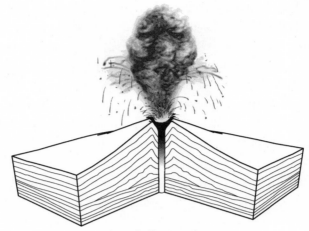

Strombolian eruption

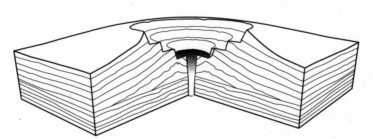

Hawaiian eruption

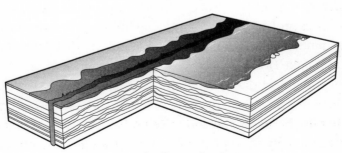

Icelandic eruption

THE NATURE MAGPIE

That is not to say Icelandic eruptions are any less disruptive. The world became very aware of this soon after a volcanic event on 14 April 2010. 250 million cubic metres of volcanic ash pumped into the sky, the plume rose over 30,000 feet above Iceland, and cloud drifted towards mainland Europe. Experts identified the fine ash as a danger to plane engines, leading to eight days of disruptive airspace closures. 107,000 flights were cancelled, millions of passengers left stranded, and the airline industry lost an estimated US$1.7 billion (£1.1 billion). At the time the only thing that seemed more dangerous than flying through ash clouds was attempting to pronounce Eyjafjallajökull. The mere thought of 'that' Icelandic volcano still has the power to give the most eloquent of newsreaders sleepless nights.

CLOUD CLASSIFICATION

'Whereas the medieval never painted a cloud but with the purpose of placing an angel upon it', art critic John Ruskin wrote in *Modern Painters* (1856), 'we have no belief that the clouds contain more than so many inches of rain or hail.' This artistic change from celestial thrones to masses of condensed water vapour was influenced by an amateur meteorologist from London. In December 1802 Luke Howard (1772–1864) delivered a lecture, 'On the Modifications of Clouds', to the Askesian Society. Since he was an unknown speaker and a manufacturing chemist by trade, the audience probably wasn't expecting much. By the end of the lecture, as Richard Hamblyn explains in *The Invention of Clouds* (2001), Howard had lifted himself to the 'realms of scientific and Romantic celebrity'. In devising a Latin nomenclature based on the Linnaean system, Howard had given 'language to nature's most ineffable and prodigal forms'; more simply, he had 'named the clouds'.

Howard introduced basic cloud types: *cirrus* (curl), *cumulus* (heap), *stratus* (spread out), *nimbus* (rain cloud) and their derivatives *cirrocumulus* and *cirrostratus*. When his work was published in the *Philosophical Magazine* in 1803, the broader significance of the cloud classification system to the science of meteorology was recognised:

> Clouds are subject to certain distinct modifications, produced by the general causes which affect all the variations of the atmosphere; they are commonly as good visible indicators of the operation of these causes, as is the countenance of the state of a person's mind or body.

This science trickled into artistic thinking. John Constable (1776–1837) argued that 'Painting is a science, and should be pursued as an enquiry into the laws of nature'. Refusing to make skies simply white sheets drawn behind objects, Constable's clouds represented an 'organ of sentiment'. In 1821 and 1822 Constable combined his meteorological interest with detailed observations recorded in his Hampstead cloud sketches. By 1823, he regarded himself as 'the man of clouds'.

Ruskin (1819–1900) had an unfavourable view of

Constable's work, which seems odd when you consider that he argued that the main role of the artist was 'truth to nature'. Perhaps unbeknown to Ruskin they both drew inspiration from Howard's meteorological ideas. Ruskin went as far as to say: 'If a general and characteristic name were needed for modern landscape art, none better could be invented than "the service of clouds".' Through *Modern Painters*, he essentially offered landscape painters a course in physical geography, ensuring that the role of clouds would not be forgotten in the future.

Below is a table of the ten basic cloud genera still used today.

Genus			Defined by
Cirrus	Ci	High Clouds	Howard, 1802
Cirrocumulus	Cc		Howard, 1802
Cirrostratus	Cs		Howard, 1802
Altocumulus	Ac	Medium Clouds	Émilien Renou, 1877
Altostratus	As		Émilien Renou, 1877
Nimbostratus	Ns		Howard, 1802
Stratocumulus	Sc	Low Clouds	Ludwig Kaemtz, 1840
Stratus	St		Howard, 1802
Cumulus	Cu		Howard 1802
Cumulonimbus	Cb		Philip Weilbach, 1880

'Nature is a mutable cloud which is always and never the same.'
—Ralph Waldo Emerson (1803–1882)

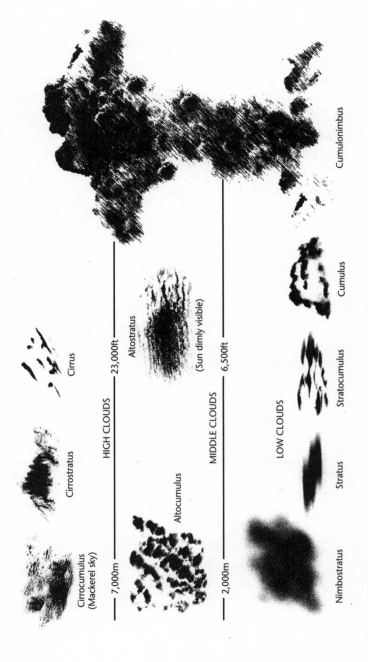

Cumulonimbus

Cumulus

Stratocumulus

Stratus

Nimbostratus

Altostratus

(Sun dimly visible)

Altocumulus

Cirrus

Cirrostratus

Cirrocumulus
(Mackerel sky)

HIGH CLOUDS

23,000ft

7,000m

MIDDLE CLOUDS

6,500ft

2,000m

LOW CLOUDS

THE NATURE MAGPIE

CLOUD APPRECIATION SOCIETY

How can anyone not be mesmerised by clouds? With one glance to the sky, daydreamers can escape the drudgery of daily life and let their imaginations run wild, cynics are presented with ever-changing harbingers of rain to grumble about to strangers, those who work the land can attempt to predict the weather, and meteorologists can do the same for a handsome wage without having to worry about wayward predictions. For *The Cloudspotter's Guide* author Gavin Pretor-Pinney, 'Nothing in nature rivals their variety and drama; nothing matches their sublime, ephemeral beauty.' Saddened by the fact that few people seemed to share his love for cloudspotting, Pretor-Pinney decided to set up the Cloud Appreciation Society in 2004. Its global membership has grown to over 31,500 members. If you are inspired by the society's manifesto below, why not become a member today?

The Manifesto of
the Cloud Appreciation Society

WE BELIEVE that clouds are unjustly maligned
and that life would be immeasurably poorer
without them.

☁

We think that they are Nature's poetry,
and the most egalitarian of her displays, since
everyone can have a fantastic view of them.

☁

We pledge to fight 'blue-sky thinking' wherever
we find it.
Life would be dull if we had to look up at
cloudless monotony day after day.

⌒

We seek to remind people that clouds are
expressions of the
atmosphere's moods, and can be read like those of
a person's countenance.

⌒

Clouds are so commonplace that their beauty
is often overlooked.
They are for dreamers and their contemplation
benefits the soul.
Indeed, all who consider the shapes they see
in them will save
on psychoanalysis bills.

⌒

And so we say to all who'll listen:
*Look up, marvel at the ephemeral beauty, and live life
with your head in the clouds!*

WHO LIKES THE RAIN?

The sunshine is overrated. It does not pitter-patter, pour
or puddle. It cannot quench thirst or soak to the bone.
It is not associated to the wonderful words, splishing,
splashing and sploshing. What is there not to like about
the rain? For those who prefer to soak up the sun, this

poem by American writer Clara Doty Bates (1838–1895) is sure to put a smile on your face on a rainy day.

Who Likes The Rain?

'I,' said the duck. 'I call it fun,
For I have my red rubbers on;
They make a little three-toed track,
In the soft, cool mud, – quack! quack!'

'I!' cried the dandelion. 'I!
My roots are thirsty, my buds are dry.'
And she lifted a tousled yellow head
Out of her green and grassy bed.

'I hope 'twill pour! I hope 'twill pour!'
Purred the tree-toad at the gray bark door,
'For, with a broad leaf for a roof,
I am perfectly waterproof.'

Sang the brook: 'I laugh at every drop.
And wish they never need to stop
Till a big, big river I grow to be,
And could find my way to the sea.'

'I,' shouted Ted, 'for I can run,
With my high-top boots and rain-coat on,
Through every puddle and runlet and pool,
I find on the road to school.'

SNOW

'The first fall of snow,' wrote the novelist J.B. Priestley (1894–1984), 'is not only an event, it is a magical event.'

In England the novelty of this natural phenomenon makes it enchanting, as does the sound of crunch-crunch-crunch which accompanies every step on the freshly whitened ground. The ability to transform landscapes, to conceal recognisable features, to be shaped into human-like forms, and indeed to make a whole nation come to a standstill all add to its magical quality. Snowflakes are even more amazing. If nature were a magician, they would be the show-stopping trick. The old adage that no two snowflakes are the same is well known; the procedure for classifying them is much less so.

Japanese physicist Ukichiro Nakaya (1900–1962) regarded snow crystals as 'letters sent from heaven', and dedicated his life to studying them. Credited with creating the first artificial snowflake in 1933, for years he worked in a purpose-built chamber that simulated snow-producing clouds. Nakaya went on to identify 41 individual morphological crystal types. Chōji Magono and Chung Woo Lee extended this to 80 in their 1966 work *Meteorological Classification of Natural Snow Crystals*.

The classification scheme used today is far less confusing. Introduced by the International Commission on Snow and Ice in 1951, it defines seven main types (plates, stellar crystals, columns, needles, spatial dendrites, capped columns, irregular forms) and three forms of frozen precipitation (graupel, ice pellets, hail).

> 'Nature is full of genius, full of divinity; so that not a snowflake escapes its fashioning hand.'
> —Henry David Thoreau, 1852

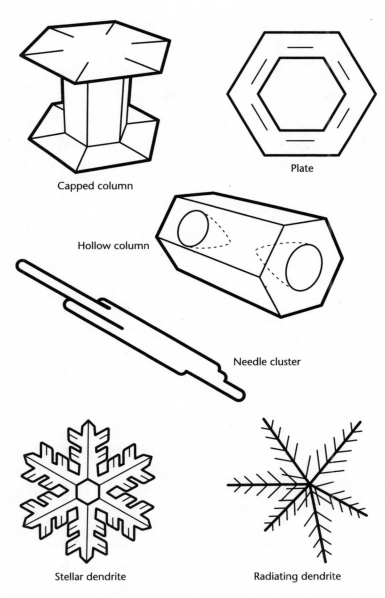

Capped column

Plate

Hollow column

Needle cluster

Stellar dendrite

Radiating dendrite

Types of snow

WEATHER WISDOM

'Earlier on today, apparently, a woman rang the BBC
and said she heard there was a hurricane on the way
... well, if you're watching, don't worry, there isn't,'
–Michael Fish, 15 October 1987

The now infamous words of BBC weatherman Michael Fish were delivered just hours before Britain was hit by its worst storm since 1703. The Great Storm of 1987 did untold damage, taking the lives of eighteen people. Weather prediction can be a challenge, even for the wisest of meteorologists. Historically, those whose livelihoods and lives depended on the weather used rhyming couplets and proverbs based on observations. Below are examples of weather lore from around the world. They may seem far-fetched, but give them a go; some are more reliable than others.

When grass is dry at morning light,
Look for rain before the night.

Red sky at night, sailor's delight,
Red sky at morning, sailors take warning.

Ants that move their eggs and climb,
Rain is coming anytime.

Trace the sky with painter's brush,
The winds around you soon will rush.

Haloes around the moon or sun
Mean that rain will surely come.

Year of snow,
Crops will grow.

Rainbow in the south, heavy rain and snow,
Rainbow in the west, little showers and dew,
Rainbow in the east, fair skies and blue.

When the donkey blows his horn,
'Tis time to house your hay and corn.

If the cock crows going to bed,
He will certainly rise with a watery head.

Sea gull, sea gull, sit on the sand,
It's never good weather while you're on the land.

Onion skins very thin,
Midwinter coming in.
Onions skins very tough,
Winter's coming cold and rough.

Moss dry, sunny sky;
Moss wet, rain you'll get.

If those nuggets of weather wisdom do not help with future
predictions, you should try and find some Mermaid's Tresses
or a Shepherd's Weatherglass. They are not expensive or
as rare as you might imagine. Mermaids Tresses, more
commonly known as Bootlace Weed (*Chorda filum*), absorb
moisture. When placed in a sheltered area, low humidity
makes it brittle, indicating the next day is likely to be dry. It
goes limp when there is dampness in the air. The Shepherd's
Weatherglass is in fact the Scarlet Pimpernel (*Anagallis
arvensis*). These small flowers close when rain is due.

GREAT HIPPOCAMPUS QUESTION

'How much doth the hideous monkey resemble us!' exclaimed Roman poet Quintus Ennius in 200BC. Humanity has long been troubled by the physical appearance, movements and behaviour of monkeys and apes. Their likeness to us is just that little too close for comfort. The suggestion we could be related remains a hideous thought to some people, even in the 21st century.

Carolus Linnaeus (1707–1778) argued that 'man is the only creature with a rational and immortal soul', but he could not 'discover scarcely any mark by which man can be distinguished from the apes'. Apes were therefore placed in the same taxonomic order as humans: primates. Distinguished palaeontologist and anatomist Richard Owen (1804–1892) did not agree. As he explained in 1844, his work on comparative anatomy of apes and man proved otherwise:

> The Chimpanzee being the highest organised quadrumanous animal and the first in the descensive scale, from Man, every difference between its anatomy and the Human exemplifies in the most instructive manner the characteristic peculiarities of the human organisation.

With the discovery of gorillas in 1847, followed by a further decade of continued research, Owen acknowledged anatomical similarities but maintained that humans held a unique position in nature. The proof of this uniqueness, according to Owen, was that the human brain had three exclusive structures: (1) a posterior lobe (which influences motor coordination); (2) a posterior horn (which extends into the occipital lobe); and (3) a hippocampus minor (which consolidates memory). With this evidence Owen proposed that the genus of homo belonged to a totally separate sub-class of mammals. He called this *Archencephala*, or 'ruling brains'. Antievolutionists delighted at such an announcement: this meant humans could not possibly be related to apes. No other biologist had presented such evidence before.

These celebrations would be short lived; anatomist Thomas Henry Huxley (1825–1895) made certain of this. Having been convinced of evolution with the publication of Charles Darwin's *On The Origin of Species* in 1859, Huxley became Darwin's most vocal and assertive supporter. His combative style and intellectual baiting soon earned him the nickname 'Darwin's Bulldog'. Huxley's own work contradicted that of Owen, demonstrating the similarity of humans to apes. More importantly, he could prove that Owen, who had a reputation for being deceitful, had made a series of major scientific errors in relation to the brain. Unleashed, Huxley wanted blood: 'Before I have done with that mendacious humbug I will nail him out, like a kite to a barn door, an example to all evil doers.'

The opportunity arose at the British Association for the Advancement of Science meeting in 1860, where they were both in attendance. The broader controversy about evolution had prompted Owen to stand and recount his theory about the human brain. When he finished, Huxley, who had not publicly spoken about this point before, categorically denied 'that the difference between the brain of the gorilla and man was so great'. He also promised to prove Owen wrong by presenting the facts. The fierce public rivalry continued. True to his word, Huxley presented a barrage of evidence from the world's leading anatomists. The argument caused great controversy; the press termed it the 'great hippocampus question'. Author Charles Kingsley (1819–1875) even parodied it as the 'great hippopotamus test' in *The Water-Babies* (1863).

The release of Huxley's *Evidence on Man's Place in Nature* in 1863 finally answered the great hippocampus question. Huxley reproduced finding of dissections, conclusively proving that all three structures were also present in apes. Unfortunately for Owen, it also 'fixed him in the history books for an egregious triplet of errors rather than his more than 600 scientific papers, many of which made significant contributions'.

> **'I viewed my fellow man not as a fallen angel, but as a risen ape.'**
> —Desmond Morris

MONKEYANA

Disputes over human uniqueness and the broader creation-evolution controversy were presented to the public through science, sensationalism and satire.

'Monkeyana' was an anonymously penned squib in the May 1861 issue of *Punch*. Headed with an image of a walking stick-wielding gorilla and a placard reading 'Am I a man and a brother?', the poem regales over decades of intellectual bickering. The author, signed off as 'Gorilla', turned out to be palaeontologist Sir Philip Egerton MP. As Egerton was a patron of Richard Owen (1804–1892), you will see why this public criticism pleased 'Darwin's Bulldog', Thomas Huxley (1825–1895).

Am I satyr or man?
Pray tell me who can,
And settle my place in the scale.
A man in ape's shape,
An anthropoid ape,
Or monkey deprived of his tail?

The *Vestiges* taught,
That all came from naught
By "development," so called, "progressive;"
That insects and worms
Assume higher forms
By modification excessive.

Then Darwin set forth
In a book of much worth,
The importance of "nature's selection;"
How the struggle for life
Is a laudable strife,
And results in "specific distinction."

Let pigeons and doves
Select their own loves,
And grant them a million of ages,
Then doubtless you'll find
They've altered their kind,
And changed into prophets and sages.

Leonard Horner relates,
That Biblical dates
The age of the world cannot trace;
That Bible tradition,
By Nile's deposition,
Is put to the right about face.

Then there's Pengelly
Who next will tell ye
That he and his colleagues of late
Find celts and shaped stones
Mixed up with cave bones
Of contemporaneous date.

Then Prestwich, he pelts
With hammers and celts
All who do not believe his relation,
That the tools he exhumes
From gravelly tombs
Date before the Mosaic creation.

Then Huxley and Owen,
With rivalry glowing,
With pen and ink rush to the scratch;

'Tis Brain *versus* Brain,
Till one of them's slain,

By JOVE! it will be a good match!
Says Owen, you can see
The brain of Chimpanzee
Is always exceedingly small,
With the hindermost "horn"
Of extremity shorn,
And no "Hippocampus" at all.

The Professor then tells 'em,
That man's "cerebellum,"
From a vertical point you can't see;
That each "convolution"
Contains a solution
Of "Archencephalic" degree.

That apes have no nose,
And thumbs for great toes,
And a pelvis both narrow and slight;
They can't stand upright,
Unless to show fight,
With 'Du Chaillu,' that chivalrous knight!

Next Huxley replies,
That Owen he lies,
And garbles his Latin quotation;
That his facts are not new,
His mistakes not a few,
Detrimental to his reputation.

"To twice slay the slain,
By dint of the Brain,
(Thus Huxley concludes his review)
Is but labour in vain,
Unproductive of gain,
And so I shall bid you 'Adieu'!"

Zoological Gardens, May, 1861
GORILLA

EVOLUTION OF EVOLUTION

Charles Darwin's (1809–1882) theory of descent with modification shook the very foundations of religion and outraged polite Victorian society. It is now widely regarded as the most influential biological work of the 19th century. Many misconceptions have become associated with the theory, one being that it appeared from nowhere as a fully formed idea in *On the Origin of Species* (1859). The work was indeed groundbreaking, but the theory had been largely developed decades earlier.

Darwin was an ardent diarist. He recorded every field observation and chronicled his ideas in volumes of notebooks. Due to this it can be proved that the evolutionary 'Tree of Life' made public in 1859, was clear in his mind as early as 1837. Accompanying the sketch in 'Red Transmutation Notebook B' Darwin scribbled:

I think case must be that one generation should have as many living as now. To do this and to have as many species in same genus (as is) requires extinction. Thus between A + B the immense gap of relation. C + B the finest gradation. B+D rather greater distinction. Thus genera would be formed. Bearing relation to ancient types with several extinct forms.

With this model for evolution, his theory was near complete by 1839. Why then did it take 20 years for Darwin to publish? Scientific caution was one factor. As evolution could not be observed directly, Darwin had to gather indirect evidence from existing research. Synthesising the work of his contemporaries and peers was an unprecedented task, requiring five years of undivided attention. Fully aware of the furore the theory would generate, the mild-mannered naturalist also feared persecution and social disgrace. Neither Darwin nor society was ready for such a revelation.

On 18 June 1858, Darwin received a letter from young naturalist Alfred Russell Wallace (1823–1913), which would prove pivotal. As he read the 20 pages describing an evolutionary mechanism, he was horrified by the similarity of the theory. In a letter to geologist Charles Lyell (1797–1875), he confided, 'All my originality, whatever it may amount to, will be smashed.' After much persuasion from his friend Lyell, Darwin agreed to present a joint paper with Wallace at the Linnean Society of London. 'On the Tendency of Species to form Varieties; and on the Perpetuation of Varieties and Species by Natural Means of Selection' generated little reaction. The following year, on 22 November 1859, *On the Origin of Species* was published.

Darwin avoided incorporating the ancestry of humans into the theory, although did hint at this in the concluding chapter. 'In the future I see open fields for far more important researches. Much light will be thrown on the origin of man and his history,' he wrote. With the publication of *The Descent of Man, and Selection in Relation to Sex* in 1871, humans finally became an official part of his broader theory. Darwin confidently mused:

> In each great region of the world the living mammals are closely related to the extinct species of the same region. It is therefore probable that Africa was formerly inhabited by extinct apes closely allied to the gorilla and chimpanzee; as these two species are now man's closest allies, it is somewhat more probable that our early progenitors lived on the African continent than elsewhere.

Although the satirists continued to mock, Darwin was pleasantly surprised that everybody was 'talking about it without being shocked'. Darwin could finally relax. The theory which had been eating away at his nerves for half a century had been accepted and welcomed by the scientific community in just twelve years.

EVOLUTION OF VERTEBRATES

The order in which the different classes of vertebrate are believed to have evolved is as follows:

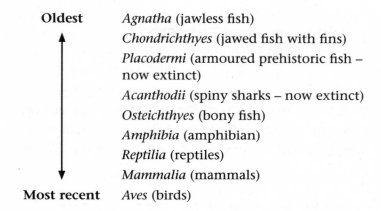

Oldest	*Agnatha* (jawless fish)
↑	*Chondrichthyes* (jawed fish with fins)
	Placodermi (armoured prehistoric fish – now extinct)
	Acanthodii (spiny sharks – now extinct)
	Osteichthyes (bony fish)
	Amphibia (amphibian)
	Reptilia (reptiles)
↓	*Mammalia* (mammals)
Most recent	*Aves* (birds)

THE MARCH OF PROGRESS

The March of Progress is arguably the world's most famous scientific illustration. It is a classic depiction of 'man's long march from apelike ancestors to sapiens', in simple visual terms. It has become an inspiration for parody, art, advertising and politics, a staple of popular culture, the icon of evolution.

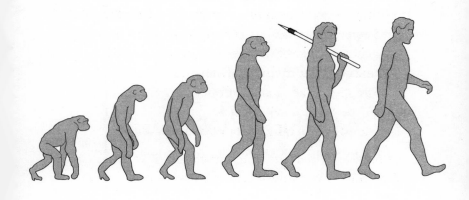

The illustration was created by Siberian-born, American-based artist Rudolph Franz Zallinger (1919–1995) in 1965. It was included in *Early Man*, a book written by anthropologist F. Clark Howell (1925–2007) as part of the Time-Life book series Life Nature Library. The original had fifteen primate figures with text spread over four pages. The simplified version has just six. From left to right:

Dryopithecus, 15 million–8 million years old

Oreopithecus, 15 million–8 million years old

Ramapithecus, 13 million–8 million year old ape and possible ancestor of modern orang-utans

Neanderthal Man, 100,000–40,000 years old

Cro-Magnon Man, 40,000–5,000 years old

Modern Man, 40,000 years to present

Many critics argue that the sequence of primate species is misleading. In his 1989 book *Wonderful Life: The Burgess Shale and the Nature of History,* evolutionary biologist Stephen Jay Gould (1941–2002) wrote:

The straitjacket of linear advance goes beyond iconography to the definition of evolution: the word itself becomes a synonym for *progress* ... life is a copiously branching bush, continually pruned by the grim reaper of extinction, not a ladder of predictable progress.

This 'straitjacket' had never been the intention of the artist or the author. It is quite clear in the original that Paranthropus (primate 7) was seen as 'an evolutionary dead end', and the timescales do not suggest direct continuity. F. Clark Howell stressed this point a year before his death during an interview with David Barringer in *i-D* magazine. 'The artist didn't intend to reduce the evolution of man to a linear sequence, but it was read that way by viewers,' explained the anthropologist. 'The graphic overwhelmed the text. It was so powerful and emotional.'

The March of Progress essentially evolved in our imaginations.

SPACE RACE

January 31, 1961. After travelling 156.5 miles up and 414 miles downrange, the sealed capsule crashes into the Atlantic Ocean and is left floating on its side. Inside the capsule he is still alive; the suit and straps have kept his body intact. Only his nose is bruised. He waits for the helicopter crewmen to find the capsule, three hours later it is hoisted to safety on the recovery ship. Peering out of the transparent panel, his dark brown eyes gaze at the sky. As the lid is removed, he grins at the commander and offers his hand. No words are exchanged, although there is much to be spoken of: the launch, crushing speeds, weightlessness, 16 minutes in space, re-entry, crash landing. No words are exchanged as the astronaut is a chimpanzee.

Ham the African-born chimpanzee (1956–1983) had been bought by the US Air Force. He and dozens of other astrochimp candidates underwent years of forced training at the Holloman Aerospace Medical Center (HAMC). As the 'best of the bunch', Ham was chosen to board the Mercury-Redstone 2 spacecraft to ensure future manned missions would be safe. He became a star, earning the distinction of being the first primate in space, beating the first human, Soviet cosmonaut Yuri Gagarin, by ten weeks. In retirement, the famous astrochimp was pampered at the National Zoo in Washington DC, then North Carolina Zoo.

Ham was neither the first nor last animal in space. Other notable examples include:

First animal (1947): Fruit flies on a US mission aboard captured German V-2 rockets.

First mammal (1949): Albert II, a rhesus monkey, was anesthetised and sent into space by the United States to test rates of radiation at altitude. He was killed by the impact of re-entry.

First dog (1957): Laika, a stray mongrel, was the first animal to orbit the earth. She was on board the Soviet satellite Sputnik 2, on a mission with no intention to return.

First cat (1963): Having been sent into space by French scientists, Felix was successfully retrieved after a parachute descent.

Record animal orbit (1966): Russian dogs Veterok and Ugolyok orbited for 22 days, a record not surpassed by humans until 1974.

EXTREME EXPEDITIONS

A desire to conquer nature runs through the veins of humanity. The Amundsen–Scott race for the South Pole (1911–1912) saw the Norwegian Antarctic expedition victorious and their British counterparts dead. Danger, adventure, courage, heroism, patriotism, deceit, and honour are all associated with the planet's most extreme places. For another British explorer of the Antarctic, Ernest Shackleton (1874–1922), the memories made starvation, frostbite and near-death worthwhile: 'We had seen God in His splendors, heard the text that Nature renders. We had reached the naked soul of man.'

The summit of Mount Everest, the world's highest peak, presented a new challenge. When asked why he wanted to climb Mount Everest, English mountaineer George Mallory (1886–1924) famously responded, 'Because it's there.' The mountain claimed his life in June 1924. It was not until 29 May 1953 that the 29,002ft summit was reached by New Zealander Edmund Hillary (1919–2008) and Nepalese Sherpa Tenzing Norgay (1914–1986). Hillary was open about his motivation, explaining, 'Nobody climbs mountains for scientific reasons. Science is used to raise money for the expeditions, but you really climb for the hell of it.' He also admitted that 'It is not the mountain we conquer but ourselves'.

Earliest conquerors of Earth's most extreme places
North Pole
21 April 1908: US explorer Frederick Cook (1865–1940). Disputed
6 April 1909: US Navy engineer Robert Peary (1856–1920). Disputed
9 May 1926: US Naval officer Richard Evelyn Byrd, Jr. (1888–1957). Disputed
12 May 1926: Norwegian explorer Roald Amundsen (1872–1928)

South Pole
14 December 1911: Norwegian team of five led by Roald Amundsen (1872–1928)
17 January 1912: British team of five led by Robert Falcon Scott (1868–1912)

Mount Everest
29 May 1953: Edmund Hillary (1919–2008) and Tenzing Norgay (1914–1986)

Oceans contain 97 per cent of the planet's water and cover 71 per cent of the Earth's surface. They also offer the final frontier for exploration, as 95 per cent of the underwater world remains virtually unexplored. The Mariana Trench in the Pacific is the deepest known point of the ocean, reaching 35,800 feet (11km, 6.8 miles). For a little perspective, if Mount Everest was placed inside the trench, there would be over 6,560 feet (2,000m) of water between the summit and surface. 'Basically,' as marine biologist Michael Vecchione recently admitted, 'we know so little about the deep sea that we don't know what we don't know.'

IDENTIFYING INDIVIDUAL TURTLES

All seven of the recognised sea turtle species (hawksbill, green, flatback, loggerhead, Kemp's ridley, olive ridley, leatherback) are listed under the Endangered Species Act. These cold-blooded creatures have to contend with predation, pollution, persecution and plastic bags in their natural environments. Recognition of individuals is vital for monitoring long-term health, behaviour and populations. Traditionally, metal or plastic tags were pierced through flippers for future identification. The disadvantage of this method is that turtles have to be handled, the tags can get damaged or lost, and may also injure them.

How else can individuals by identified? 'Surely they all look the same?' is the usual response. Scientists have come up with the answer – by looking at their faces. Conservation group Turtle Trax have photographed the profiles of visiting turtles of Honokowai, Hawaii since 1989. Over the years, comparisons of the scale, shape, pattern and arrangement on the cheek has allowed individuals to be traced. Almost 700 individual turtles were recorded and named by 2004.

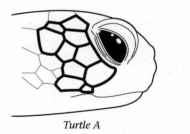
Turtle A

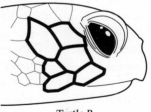
Turtle B

The distinct patterns on turtles' cheeks, which remain the same over time, have been used to successfully monitor individuals.

An academic team led by Julia Reisser reproduced their findings of this method in *Endangered Species Research* (2008). Their paper highly recommended adopting the method as a way of reducing intrusive tagging, concluding:

> The validation of photo-ID as a suitable path in individual recognition would decrease the need for intentional capture of cheloniid turtles, reduce bias in behavioral studies, increase the number of catalogued individuals (for a potentially higher time interval), and thus provide easily obtainable data for studies in nesting beaches and foraging areas.

'That will be £12.99 please. Would you like a bag?'

As a former bookseller the request for a paper bag rather than plastic, 'to help save the planet', always made me smile. We were of course standing in a graveyard for trees, reincarnated by the thousands of imaginations imprinted upon the pages. With reusable fabric bags on the rise, plastic ones are becoming even more frowned upon. Of course, they serve their purpose as water-resistant carriers, but it is becoming clear that irresponsible disposal kills.

Plastic pollution is a massive problem in our oceans, accounting for up to 80 per cent of the waste. Sea turtles regularly mistake floating bags for jellyfish, eat them and die. In 2009 a green turtle rescued in Florida went on to defecate plastic for one month, expelling 74 foreign objects.

This plastic-pooping sea turtle was lucky to survive. 'Sea turtles,' Wallace J. Nichols points out, 'are now sadly the poster animal for impacts of our throw-away society on endangered species.'

The rejection of plastic bags may not save the planet, but it may help save turtles.

SOLITUDE

Nature is widely valued for being untouched by humanity and uninterrupted by mundane commercial routines. Wild places offer solitude, an escape from modern life, inspiration. Everyone has their own personal connection with nature. Some choose to go for a walk in the woods, others prefer scuba diving, bird spotting, camping in a national park, even big game hunting. We all have our own ways of experiencing nature. Few, however, go to the extreme of escaping civilisation and living alone in the wild. Three individuals who did make this decision had very different experiences.

New England Transcendentalist **Henry David Thoreau** (1817–1862) was largely unknown to the public during his lifetime. After death, his writing had a major influence on environmental, social and political thinking. Thoreau is largely remembered for *Walden; or, Life in the Woods* (1854), a memoir which recounts his experiment of living in an isolated cabin near Walden Pond, Concord, Massachusetts. Although his cabin was only 2 miles (3km) from town, he relinquished all luxuries, lived off the land and recorded his life of hermitude.

Of nature, Thoreau wrote:

> I love Nature partly *because* she is not man, but a
> retreat from him. None of his institutions control
> or pervade her. There a different kind of right pre-
> vails. In her midst I can be glad with an entire glad-
> ness. If this world were all man, I could not stretch
> myself, I should lose all hope. He is constraint, she
> is freedom to me … What he touches he taints. In
> thought he moralizes. One would think that no
> free, joyful labor was possible to him. How infinite
> and pure the least pleasure of which Nature is basis,
> compared with the congratulation of mankind!

After two years, two months and two days, Thoreau
returned to civilisation. His friend and mentor Ralph
Waldo Emerson (1803–1882) welcomed him back to his
family home in Concord.

Christopher McCandless (1968–1992) called himself Alexander Supertramp. Inspired by nature philosophers such as Thoreau, the graduate was disenchanted
by material society and looking for adventure. He hitch-
hiked from North Dakota to Alaska, then lived alone,
foraging and hunting in the Alaskan wilderness. After
113 days of solitude, McCandless died of starvation. His
life went on to be fictionalised (and romanticised) by
Jon Krakauer in the 1996 book *Into the Wild*, and the
2007 Sean Penn-directed movie adaptation.

In the 1980s, failed actor, recovering addict and
self-proclaimed eco-warrior **Timothy Treadwell**
(1957–2003) was searching for something to make his

life meaningful. In the summer of 1989 Treadwell visited Alaska for the first time, where he had a close encounter with a brown bear:

> The encounter was like looking into a mirror. I gazed into the face of a kindred soul, a being that was potentially lethal, but in reality was just as frightened as I was.

This was a life-changing moment. The meaning Treadwell had been searching for presented itself in the form of a grizzly bear. As a result he chose to visit the Alaskan wilderness every summer to live with wild bears – an unusual decision for an amateur naturalist with rudimentary survival skills. Undeterred, he named the bears he followed, spoke to them, photographed them and observed their behaviour, all at close proximity. It was only a matter of time before the media became interested. The release of Treadwell's 1997 book, *Among Grizzlies: Living with Wild Bears in Alaska*, brought him recognition and fame. He starred in *The Grizzly Diaries* on the Discovery Channel, and was interviewed on primetime television. 'We're not going to open a newspaper one day and read about you being eaten by a bear, are we?' David Letterman quipped in 2001.

At the end of his thirteenth summer with wild grizzlies, Timothy Treadwell and his girlfriend Amie Huguenard were killed and eaten by a bear.

> **'I love not man the less, but Nature more'**
> —**Lord Byron (1788–1824)**

NATIONAL PARKS

Solitude, savageness, danger, bewilderment and terror were some of the adjectives used to describe the American wilderness in the 18th century. Today, the National Park Service defines wilderness as 'rare, wild places where one can retreat from civilization, reconnect with the Earth, and find healing, meaning and significance.' Quite a transformation! Attitudes in America started changing in the early 19th century. Literary influences from European Romantics merged with a growing realisation that the frontier experience could not continue without wilderness.

The California Gold Rush (1848–1859) attracted thousands of gold seekers to the region from across the world. Increased numbers and commercial interests from mining and lumber industries were seen as threats to the pristine nature of Yosemite Valley. American Unitarian minister Thomas Starr King (1824–1864) was the first person of influence to publicly celebrate this. During his extended trip to the area in 1860, he wrote of the El Capitan rock formation, 'A more majestic object than this rock, I expect never to see on this planet. Great is granite, and the Yo-Semite is its prophet!'

Pressure from Starr King and others led to the Yosemite Land Grant, signed by President Abraham Lincoln on 30 June 1864. This legislation ceded California the Yosemite Valley and Mariposa Big Tree Grove 'upon the express conditions that the premises shall be held for public use, resort, and recreation'. The following year Frederick Law Olmsted (1822–1903) outlined his broader vision of national parks, warning that 'all places favorable in scenery to the recreation of the mind and body will be closed against the mass of the people', unless the government intervened. It is these events which set the precedent for the creation of the first national park in 1872, Yellowstone.

Back in California, a Scottish-born American preservationist had made the state park his home, and was publicly exalting the beauty and spiritual importance of wilderness. 'No temple made with hands can compare with Yosemite ... The grandest of all special temples of Nature,' exclaimed John Muir (1838–1914). His preservationist views and recommendations led to the creation of Yosemite national park in 1890.

Theodore 'Teddy' Roosevelt (1858–1919), known by many as the 'Conservationist President', recognised the importance of wild country to future generations:

> There can be nothing in the world more beautiful than the Yosemite, the groves of the giant sequoias and redwoods, the Canyon of the Colorado, the Canyon of the Yellowstone, the Three Tetons; and our people should see to it that they are preserved for their children and their children's children forever, with their majestic beauty all marred.

This support paved the way for the establishment of the National Park Service in 1916. A century later, this government agency manages 398 units, 59 of which are designated national parks.

According to American novelist and historian Wallace Stegner (1909–1993), 'National parks are the best idea we ever had. Absolutely American, absolutely democratic, they reflect us at our best rather than our worst.' It would be difficult to find many people who disagree with this sentiment.

Below are listed the 59 United States National Parks, by date of park status designation.

1872	Yellowstone	**1962**	Petrified Forest
1890	Yosemite	**1964**	Canyonlands
	Sequoia	**1966**	Guadalupe Mountains
1899	Mount Rainier	**1968**	North Cascades
1902	Crater Lake		Redwood
1903	Wind Cave	**1971**	Capitol Reef
1906	Mesa Verde		Voyageurs
1910	Glacier	**1978**	Arches
1915	Rocky Mountain		Theodore Roosevelt
1916	Lassen Volcanic	**1980**	Channel Islands
1919	Grand Canyon		Biscayne
	Zion		Denali
1921	Hot Springs		Katmai
1926	Great Smoky Mountains		Glacier Bay
	Shenandoah		Gates of the Arctic
	Mammoth Cave		Kenai Fjords
1928	Bryce Canyon		Kobuk Valley
1929	Acadia		Lake Clark
	Badlands		Wrangell St Elias
	Grand Teton	**1986**	Great Basin
1930	Carlsbad Caverns	**1988**	National Park of
1931	Isle Royale		American Samoa
1934	Everglades	**1992**	Dry Tortugas
1935	Big Bend	**1994**	Death Valley
1938	Olympic		Saguaro
1940	Kings Canyon		Joshua Tree
1956	Zion	**1999**	Black Canyon of the
	Virgin Islands		Gunnison
1960	Haleakala	**2000**	Cuyahoga Valley
1961	Hawaii Volcanoes	**2003**	Congaree
		2004	Great Sand Dunes

> 'Yosemite is a real place in nature – but its venerated status as a sacred landscape and a national symbol is very much a human invention ... To protect the nature that is all around us, we must think long and hard about the nature we carry inside our heads.'
> —William Cronon, 1995

DAM HETCH HETCHY!

Yosemite National Park became the battleground for American environmentalism in the 20th century. The San Francisco earthquake of 1906 and subsequent rebuilding led to calls for a new reservoir to provide more reliable water supplies to the city. The Hetch Hetchy Valley was the proposed site. American forester and conservationist Gifford Pinchot (1865–1946), stated:

> I am fully persuaded that ... the injury ... by substituting a lake for the present swampy floor of the valley ... is altogether unimportant compared with the benefits to be derived from its use as a reservoir.

Sierra Club founder and preservationist John Muir was adamantly opposed to the scheme, and desperate to protect the wild beauty of the valley:

> The temple destroyers, devotees of ravaging commercialism, seem to have a perfect contempt for Nature, and instead of lifting their eyes to the God

of the Mountains, lift them to the Almighty Dollar. Dam Hetch Hetchy! As well dam for water-tanks the people's cathedrals and churches, for no holier temple has ever been consecrated by the heart of man.

After years of national debate, President Woodrow Wilson (1856–1924) authorised the construction of the dam in 1913. Well-planned management of natural resources had been chosen over preserving scenic wilderness. The valley would be flooded. Muir was devastated but took consolation that 'the conscience of the whole country' had 'been aroused from sleep' by the controversy. The O'Shaughnessy Dam was completed, at a cost of $100 million, in 1923, and the reservoir system was in use by 1934.

The Hetch Hetchy debate has recently resurfaced. Although water from the reservoir serves 2.4 million Californians, there are calls from environmental groups to drain the 117-billion-gallon reservoir and restore the valley.

DAM

The beaver is one of natural world's most extraordinary builders. Their life is dedicated to constructing, repairing and enlarging the dam and lodge which provide food and shelter. Beavers build dams to enlarge the underwater habitat available to them in the winter months. It essentially creates a deep pond that will not freeze, thus providing storage for winter food and underwater access to their lodge throughout the year. Their cache often includes branches from aspen, birch, poplar, willow, and roots of aquatic plants such as cattails. According to the Canadian Wildlife Federation's public announcement website Hinterland Who's Who, 'Half a hectare of aspen will support one beaver for a year.'

A beaver can cut down an average of 216 trees a year. It can fell trees up to about 40cm (16in) in diameter. The beaver's efficiency is such that trees can be felled in less than fifteen minutes. The world's biggest beaver dam measures 2,790ft (850m) in length. Located in Wood Buffalo National Park in Northern Alberta, Canada, it is twice the length of the Hoover Dam, and can be seen from space. It is thought the beavers started construction in the 1970s.

BEAVER AS NATIONAL SYMBOL

The history of Canada is inseparable from the history of the North American beaver (*Castor canadensis*). Having first explored the vast, largely uninhabited tracts of land in the late 15th century, Europeans soon spread in pursuit of the fur-bearing rodent. Commercial trapping areas, trading posts, settlements and even the Beaver Wars (1640s–1680s) later followed.

Beavers became acknowledged in Canadian culture. Corporate fur traders the Hudson's Bay Company used four beavers, two moose and a red fox in their coat of arms in 1671 – an emblem that they retain to this day. The animal was included in the City of Montréal armorial bearings in 1833 and also appeared on the first Canadian postage stamp, the 'three-penny beaver', in 1851.

The soft underfur of the beaver's pelt proved popular in the fashion industry, as it was particularly useful for making felt. Beaver fur coats and hats clad the most respectable of gentlemen. By the 20th century the beaver, which once had an estimated population of over 60 million, had been decimated by the trade, leaving roughly 100,000.

From the late 1920s awareness of the plight of the species was raised by conservationists, most notably Grey Owl (see page 160). As a result, beaver trapping was prohibited in the 1930s. Reintroduction schemes were also implemented in areas where the fur trade had wiped out the species. A recovery was soon under way. The Prince Albert National Park, for example, capped the population at 500 in 1935; any surplus were relocated. By 1952, the population had risen to almost 15,000. This resurgence took place on a national scale.

The shared past of Canada and the resilient beaver was acknowledged on 24 March 1975 when the animal became the 'symbol of the sovereignty of Canada', by Royal assent. Yet despite this journey, the beaver, now boasting an estimated population of 20 million, is still not appreciated by all. In October 2011, Senator Nicole Eaton suggested an alternative symbol:

'Many accuse the dentally defective rat of being a nuisance that wreaks havoc on farmlands, roads, lakes, streams and tree plantations … It is high time that the beaver step aside as a Canadian emblem or, at the least, share the honour with the stately polar bear… A country's symbols are not constant and can change over time as long as they reflect the ethos of the people and the spirit of the nation … The polar bear, with its strength, courage, resourcefulness and dignity is perfect for the part.'

This call for an 'emblem makeover' sparked a broader, albeit playful debate about the perception of Canadian national identity. 'Beaver or bear? Fur flies over Canadian sense of identity,' Lorraine Mallinder wrote, for *BBC News Magazine*. The respective animals' qualities were then put alongside each other, with the heading 'Cutie v. Bully':

Beaver: monogamous, lives with family, herbivorous, nocturnal, short-sighted, close relative of the squirrel, females as large as males, predators include coyotes, wolves and bears.

Polar bear: largest land carnivore, 42 teeth, lives alone, sharp-sighted, can smell a seal from a mile away, males twice the size of females, has been known to kill and eat humans, no predators.

The small, pleasant, hard-working, resilient rodent was set against the strong, powerful, feared and respected bear. The latter animal does seem more in-keeping with Canada's national anthem, which extols 'The True

North, strong and free', but the thought of somehow acquiring those strengths and being seen differently on the global stage is wishful thinking.

The debate rumbles on. 'Has there ever been a national symbol more loathed or misunderstood?' pondered Frances Backhouse in the December 2012 issue of *Canadian Geographic*. The magazine proudly shared its allegiance again in February 2013, stating through social media, 'We proudly stand behind the beaver as Canada's national animal. Though we do hold the polar bear in high regard.'

Admittedly, Canada is home to roughly 16,000 polar bears – that's over two thirds of the global population. They also desperately need international recognition in their own right to survive. But, as a species, they have become a symbol of scavenging, of homelessness, of charity. Why would anyone want that as a national symbol? If I were Canadian I would be proud of the beaver.

GREY OWL

Grey Owl was the name Englishman Archibald Belaney (1888–1938) adopted when he took on a First Nations identity on immigrating to Canada. One-time fur trapper Belaney was influenced by Ojibwe culture, and lived their beliefs as Grey Owl. He realised that trapping, shooting and poisoning fur-bearing animals would eventually result to their demise, and opposed the 'commodification of all living things'. He and his two pet beavers, Rawhide and Jelly Roll, shot to fame in 1928, appearing in the silent movie *Beaver People*. This was the first motion picture of beavers in their natural setting. Three years later he became 'caretaker of park animals' at Riding Mountain National Park in Manitoba. As a conservationist and writer, Grey Owl reminded people 'that you belong to nature, and not it to you'. He is now widely appreciated as the one of the 'most effective apostles of the wilderness,' and saviour of the beaver.

A later Englishman to learn from the Ojibwe was Shaun Ellis, who went on to write *The Man Who Lives with Wolves* (2010). In a 2007 interview he said, 'It was really evident that what we were learning from a scientific point of view from wolves wasn't very much. The Native Americans I lived with knew far more about wolves than we ever did. I believe it was because they had the time to live alongside these creatures, to share their world.'

GO'BBLES AMERICA

Like the stars and stripes, the bald eagle (*Haliaeetus leucocephalus*) is an internationally recognised symbol of the USA. Chosen for its strength, long life, beauty and indigenous status in North America, it is now inseparable from the national persona. Yet it once had an avian contender. If founding father Benjamin Franklin (1706–1790) had had his way, a far less attractive bird may now be the celebrated national symbol.

Although Franklin never publicly voiced his opposition, this letter to his daughter reveals all:

For my own part I wish the Bald Eagle had not been chosen the Representative of our Country. He is a Bird of bad moral Character. He does not get his Living honestly. You may have seen him perched on some dead Tree near the River, where, too lazy to fish for himself, he watches the Labour of the Fishing Hawk; and when that diligent Bird has at length taken a Fish, and is bearing it to his Nest for the Support of his Mate and young Ones, the Bald Eagle pursues him and takes it from him.

With all this Injustice, he is never in good Case but like those among Men who live by Sharping & Robbing he is generally poor and often very lousy. Besides he is a rank Coward: The little King Bird not bigger than a Sparrow attacks him boldly and drives him out of the District. He is therefore by no means a proper Emblem for the brave and honest Cincinnati of America who have driven all the King birds from our Country ...

I am on this account not displeased that the Figure [on the United States coat of arms] is not known as a Bald Eagle, but looks more like a Turkey. For the Truth the Turkey is in Comparison a much more respectable Bird, and withal a true original Native of America ... He is besides, though a little vain & silly, a Bird of Courage, and would not hesitate to attack a Grenadier of the British Guards who should presume to invade his Farm Yard with a red Coat on.

January 26, 1784

The 'vain & silly' turkey did not become the country's representative, but Americans have developed a taste for this 'respectable' bird. According to the National Turkey Federation, more than 219 million turkeys were consumed in the United States in 2011. Of those, an estimated 46 million were eaten at Thanksgiving, 22 million at Christmas and 19 million at Easter.

THE UNITED STATES OF ANIMALS

Unlike the national avian symbol of America, the official animals of the 50 individual states are far less familiar to those who do not reside in them. Which state, for example, chose the California Gull as their official bird? What is the most designated mammal? Which European insects have been embraced across America? The official amphibian of Louisiana is what? With the following list of official state-designated amphibians, birds, insects and mammals you will be able you confidently answer these questions. As you venture from state to state the geography of animals found across America takes shape. Approach this list as a puzzle of the United States of Animals.

Alabama Amphibian: Red Hills salamander; bird: northern flicker, wild turkey (game); insect: monarch butterfly; mammal: American black bear, racking horse (domestic); reptile: Alabama red-bellied turtle.

Alaska Amphibian: (none); bird: Willow Ptarmigan; insect: Four-Spotted Skimmer Dragonfly; mammal: Moose, Bowhead whale, Alaskan Malamute (domestic); reptile: (none).

Arizona   Amphibian: Arizona Tree Frog; bird: Cactus Wren; insect: Two-Tailed Swallowtail; mammal: Ring-tailed cat; reptile: Arizona ridge-nosed rattlesnake.

Arkansas   Amphibian: (none); bird: Northern Mockingbird; insect: European honey bee, Diana Fritillary Butterfly; mammal: White-tailed deer; reptile: (none).

California   Amphibian: (none); bird: California Quail; insect: California Dogface Butterfly; mammal: California grizzly bear, Gray whale; reptile: Desert tortoise.

Colorado   Amphibian: Western Tiger Salamander; bird: Lark Bunting; insect: Colorado Hairstreak Butterfly; mammal: Rocky Mountain bighorn sheep; reptile: Western painted turtle.

Connecticut   Amphibian: (none); bird: American Robin; insect: European mantis; Mammal: Sperm whale; reptile: (none).

Delaware   Amphibian: (none); bird: Blue Hen Chicken; insect: 7-spotted ladybug, Eastern Tiger Swallowtail; mammal: Gray fox; reptile: (none).

Florida   Amphibian: (none); bird: Northern Mockingbird; insect: Zebra Longwing; mammal: Florida panther, Manatee, Atlantic bottlenose dolphin, Florida Cracker Horse (domestic); reptile: American alligator, Loggerhead sea turtle.

Georgia   Amphibian: American Green Tree Frog; bird: Brown Thrasher, Bobwhite Quail (game); insect: European honey bee, Eastern Tiger Swallowtail; mammal: Right whale; reptile: Gopher tortoise.

Hawaii   Amphibian: (none); bird: Hawaiian Goose (Nēnē); insect: Kamehameha butterfly; mammal: Hawaiian monk seal, Humpback whale; reptile: (none).

Idaho   Amphibian: (none); bird: Mountain Bluebird; insect: Monarch Butterfly; mammal: Appaloosa horse (domestic); reptile: (none).

Illinois   Amphibian: Eastern Tiger Salamander; bird: Northern Cardinal; insect: Monarch Butterfly; mammal: White-tailed deer; reptile: Painted turtle.

Indiana   Amphibian: (none); bird: Northern Cardinal; insect: (none); mammal: (none); reptile: (none).

Iowa   Amphibian: (none); bird: American Goldfinch; insect: (none); mammal: (none); reptile: (none).

Kansas   Amphibian: Barred Tiger Salamander; bird: Western Meadowlark; insect: European honey bee; mammal: American bison; reptile: Ornate box turtle.

Kentucky   Amphibian: (none); bird: Northern Cardinal; insect: Viceroy Butterfly; mammal: Eastern gray squirrel, Thoroughbred (domestic); reptile: (none).

Louisiana   Amphibian: American Green Tree Frog; bird: Brown Pelican; insect: European honey bee; mammal: Black bear, Catahoula Leopard Dog (domestic); reptile: American alligator.

Maine   Amphibian: (none); bird: Black-capped Chickadee; insect: European honey bee; mammal: moose, Maine Coon cat (domestic); reptile: (none).

Maryland Amphibian: (none); bird: Baltimore Oriole; insect: Baltimore Checkerspot Butterfly; mammal: Thoroughbred (domestic horse), Chesapeake Bay Retriever (domestic dog), Calico cat (domestic cat); reptile: Diamondback terrapin.

Massachusetts Amphibian: (none); bird: Black-capped Chickadee, Wild Turkey (game); insect: 7-spotted ladybug; mammal: Right whale, Morgan horse (domestic), Tabby cat (domestic), Boston Terrier (domestic); reptile: Garter snake.

Michigan Amphibian: (none); bird: American Robin; insect: (none); mammal: White-tailed deer; reptile: Painted turtle.

Minnesota Amphibian: Northern Leopard Frog; bird: Common Loon; insect: Monarch Butterfly; mammal: (none); reptile: (none).

Mississippi Amphibian: (none); bird: Northern Mockingbird, Wood duck (waterfowl); insect: European honey bee, Spicebush Swallowtail; mammal: White-tailed deer, Atlantic bottlenose dolphin; reptile: American alligator.

Missouri Amphibian: North American Bullfrog; bird: Eastern Bluebird; insect: European honey bee; mammal: Missouri mule, Missouri fox trotting horse (domestic); reptile: Three-toed box turtle.

Montana Amphibian: (none); bird: Western Meadowlark; insect: Mourning Cloak Butterfly; mammal: Grizzly bear; reptile: (none).

Nebraska Amphibian: (none); bird: Western Meadowlark; insect: European honey bee; mammal: White-tailed deer; reptile: (none).

Nevada   Amphibian: (none); bird: Mountain Bluebird; insect: (none); mammal: Desert bighorn sheep; reptile: Desert tortoise.

New Hampshire   Amphibian: Red-spotted Newt; bird: Purple Finch; insect: 7-spotted ladybug, Karner Blue Butterfly; mammal: White-tailed deer, Chinook (domestic dog); reptile: (none).

New Jersey   Amphibian: (none); bird: Eastern Goldfinch; insect: European honey bee; mammal: Horse (domestic); reptile: (none).

New Mexico   Amphibian: New Mexico Spadefoot Toad; bird: Roadrunner; insect: Tarantula hawk wasp, Sandia Hairstreak Butterfly; mammal: American black bear; reptile: New Mexico whiptail lizard.

New York   Amphibian: (none); bird: Eastern Bluebird; insect: 9-spotted ladybug; mammal: Beaver; reptile: common snapping turtle.

North Carolina   Amphibian: (none); bird: Northern Cardinal; insect: European honey bee, Eastern Tiger Swallowtail; mammal: Gray squirrel, Plott Hound (domestic dog); reptile: Eastern box turtle.

North Dakota   Amphibian: (none); bird: Western Meadowlark; insect: (none); mammal: Nokota horse (domestic); reptile: (none).

Ohio   Amphibian: Spotted Salamander; bird: Northern Cardinal; insect: 7-spotted ladybug; mammal: White-tailed deer; reptile: Northern black racer.

Oklahoma   Amphibian: North American Bullfrog; bird:

Scissor-tailed Flycatcher; insect: European honey bee, Black Swallowtail Butterfly; mammal: Bison, White-tailed deer, Raccoon; reptile: Common collared lizard.

Oregon   Amphibian: (none); bird: Western Meadowlark; insect: Oregon Swallowtail Butterfly; mammal: Beaver; reptile: (none).

Pennsylvania   Amphibian: (none); bird: Ruffed Grouse; insect: Pennsylvania firefly; mammal: White-tailed deer, Great Dane (domestic dog); reptile: (none).

Rhode Island   Amphibian: (none); bird: Rhode Island Red Chicken; insect: (none); mammal: (none); reptile: (none).

South Carolina   Amphibian: Spotted Salamander; bird: Carolina Wren, Wild Turkey (game); insect: Carolina mantis, Eastern Tiger Swallowtail; mammal: White-tailed deer, Atlantic bottlenose dolphin, Right whale, Boykin spaniel (domestic dog), Mule, Marsh Tacky (domestic horse); reptile: Loggerhead sea turtle.

South Dakota   Amphibian: (none); bird: Ring-necked Pheasant; insect: European honey bee; mammal: Coyote; reptile: (none).

Tennessee   Amphibian: Tennessee Cave Salamander; bird: Northern Mockingbird, Bobwhite Quail (game); insect: Common eastern firefly, 7-spotted ladybug, European honey bee, Zebra Swallowtail Butterfly; mammal: Raccoon, Tennessee walking horse (domestic); reptile: Eastern box turtle.

Texas   Amphibian: Texas Toad; bird: Northern Mockingbird; insect: Monarch Butterfly; mammal: Nine-banded Armadillo,

Texas Longhorn (domestic cattle), Mexican Free-tailed Bat, Blue Lacy (domestic dog), American quarter horse (domestic); reptile: Texas horned lizard.

Utah   Amphibian: (none); bird: California Gull; insect: European honey bee; mammal: Rocky Mountain elk; reptile: (none).

Vermont   Amphibian: Northern Leopard Frog; bird: Hermit Thrush; insect: European honey bee, Monarch Butterfly; mammal: Morgan horse (domestic); reptile: Painted turtle.

Virginia   Amphibian: (none); bird: Northern Cardinal; insect: Tiger Swallowtail Butterfly; mammal: Virginia big-eared bat, American Foxhound (domestic dog); reptile: (none).

Washington   Amphibian: Washington Pacific Tree Frog; bird: American Goldfinch; insect: Green Darner Dragonfly; mammal: Olympic marmot, Orca; reptile: (none).

West Virginia   Amphibian: (none); bird: Northern Cardinal; insect: European honey bee, Monarch Butterfly; mammal: Black bear; reptile: Timber rattlesnake.

Wisconsin   Amphibian: (none); bird: American Robin; insect: (none); mammal: American Badger, White-tailed deer, Dairy cow (domestic), American water spaniel (domestic dog); reptile: (none).

Wyoming   Amphibian: (none); bird: Western Meadowlark; insect: European honey bee; mammal: Bison; reptile: Horned lizard.

GREAT LAKES

The Great Lakes are the largest body of fresh water on Earth, containing 21 per cent of the world's surface fresh water. The basin is home to 30.7 million Americans and 8.5 million Canadians. It accounts for 7 per cent of American farm production and almost 25 per cent of Canadian agricultural production, and fishing there (sport, commercial and Native American) represents a US$4 billion-a-year industry.

Superior is the deepest and has the largest volume: 2,900 cubic miles (12,000km^3).

Michigan is the second largest at 1,180 cubic miles (4,900km^3) and the only Great Lake entirely within the United States.

Huron the third largest by volume: 850 cubic miles (3,500km^3).

Erie is the smallest by volume at 116 cubic miles (480km^3), and the shallowest.

Ontario is second smallest by volume at 393 cubic miles (1,640km^3).

A useful mnemonic device for remembering the lakes in order from west to east is 'See My Horse Eat Oats' – Superior, Michigan, Huron, Erie, Ontario.

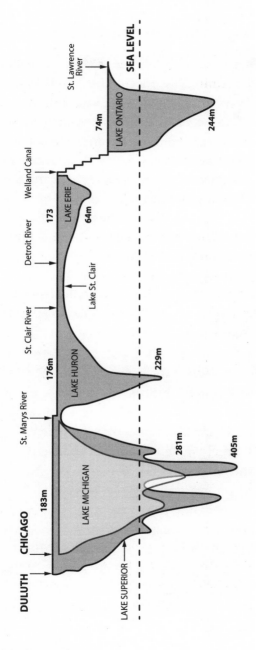

Profile of the Great Lakes

A DAY IN THE LIFE OF GILBERT WHITE

Gilbert White (1720–1793), the English parson-naturalist, is widely regarded as one of the pioneers of ecology. Rather than being drawn to grand, awe-inspiring natural environments or the perfectly manicured gardens of English landed estate, White connected with the fauna and flora of his Selborne parish in Hampshire on a daily basis. His approach was pioneering. As Welsh naturalist Ronald Lockley (1903–2000) noted: 'White saw nature with … the trained eye of scientist and countryman, having the restless intelligence of the one, and the contented homeliness and simplicity of the other, and the essential honesty of both.'

From 1767 White recorded his daily observations, sharing them in ongoing correspondence with distinguished naturalists Thomas Pennant (1726–1798) and Daines Barrington (1728–1800). These letters were published as *The Natural History and Antiquities of Selborne* in 1789, a title which continues to captivate readers in the 21st century. Its enduring influence is epitomised by the words of acclaimed nature writer Richard Mabey: 'More than any other single book it has shaped our everyday view of the relations between man and nature.'

This is no overstatement – the seemingly mundane everyday experiences are something everyone can relate to. London-based animator and cartoonist Sydney Padua explains, 'I once typed out 40 years' worth of the journals of the 18th-century naturalist Gilbert White, for no particular reason. They are absolutely lovely.'

The fruits of Padua's labour are now available online

(naturalhistoryofselborne.com), allowing readers to immerse themselves in White's writings and even to search for entries on specific dates. The entries below were all made by Gilbert White on his birthday, 18 June – they epitomise the importance of observing and the fleeting and varied nature of life:

1768 *July 18.* The country is drenched with wet, and quantities of hay were spoiled.

1769 *July 18.* Moor-buzzard, milvus aeruginosus, has young. It builds in low shrubs on wild heaths. Five young.

1772 *July 18.* Frequent sprinklings, but not enough all day to lay the dust. The dry fit has lasted six weeks this day.

1773 *July 18.* Loud thunder shower. Mrs Snooke of Ringmere near Lewes had a coach-horse killed by this tempest: the horse was at grass just before the house.

1777 *July 18.* Swifts dash & frolick about, & seem to be teaching their young the use of their wings. Thatched my rick of meadow-hay with the damaged St foin instead of straw. Bees begin gathering at three o'clock in the morning: Swallows are stirring at half hour after two.

1778 *July 18.* We have never had rain enough to lay the dust since saturday June 13: now five weeks. By watering the fruit-trees we have procured much young wood. The thermometer belonging to my brother Thomas White of South Lambeth was in the most shady part of his garden on July 5th & July 14: *up at 88*, a degree of heat not very common even at Gibraltar!! July 5: Thermr at Lyndon in Rutland 85.

1781 *July 18*. Bramshot-place Lapwings haunt the uplands still. Farmers complain that their wheat is blited. At Bramshot-place, the house of Mr Richardson, in the wilderness near the stream, grows wild, & in plenty, *Sorbus aucuparia*, the *quicken-tree*, or *mountain-ash*, *Rhamnus frangula*, *berry-bearing alder*; & *Teucrium scorodonia*, *wood-sage*, & whortle-berries. The soil is sandy. In the garden at Dowland's, the seat, lately, of Mr Kent, stands a large *Liriodendrum tulipifera*, or *tulip-tree*, which was in flower. The soil is poor sand; but produces beautiful pendulous *Larches*. Mr R's garden, tho' a sand, abounds in fruit, & in all manner of good & forward kitchen-crops. Many China-asters this spring seeded themselves there, and were forward; some cucumber-plants also grew-up of themselves from the seeds of a rejected cucumber thrown aside last autumn. The well at Downland's is 130 feet deep; at Bramshot place [...] Mr R's garden is at an average a fortnight before mine.

1785 *July 18*. Savoys & artichokes over-run with aphides. The Fly-catcher in the vine sits on her eggs, & the cock feeds her. She has four eggs.

1786 *July 18*. Gathered & preserved some Rasps.

1788 *July 18*. Fly-catcher feeds his sitting hen, Mrs H.W., Bessy, & Lucy came.

1790 *July 18*. Mrs Clement & daughters came.

1792 *July 18*. Men cut their meadows. Mr Churton came.

> 'See, Selborne spreads her boldest beauties round.
> The varied valley, and the mountain ground,
> Wildly majestic! What is all the pride,
> Of flats, with loads of ornaments supplied?—
> Unpleasing, tasteless, impotent expense,
> Compared with Nature's rude magnificence.'
>
> —Gilbert White

'INTESTINES OF THE EARTH'

There is something about earthworms which evokes memories of childhood. Digging holes in the garden to make mud pies, uncovering the silent tubes of flesh from the soil, watching in amazement as their limbless bodies wriggle on your hand. At school they were the perfect accomplices for teasing squeamish classmates. 'Nobody likes me, everybody hates me, think I'll go eat worms … Big fat juicy ones, little slimy skinny ones, hope they don't have germs!' would echo across the playground, followed by shrieks, and scenes of mischievous children dangling creatures into their mouths.

Their otherworldly appearance never ceases to amaze. As tubular annelids they consist of over 100 segments, each containing muscles and outer bristles called setae. This allows movement. With no eyes, ears, or lungs, they rely on light receptors and vibrations to sense surroundings, and breathe through their skin. Five heart-like structures, close to the head end (prostomium), pump blood around the body. Without these the creature will not survive. Cutting a worm in half, therefore, does not create two living worms, just a shorter worm which will regenerate a new rear end.

Earthworms are far more than mere playthings or fishing bait. Aristotle (384–322BC) described them as 'intestines of the earth', Gilbert White (1720–1793) applauded their role as 'great promoters of vegetation' and Charles Darwin (1809–1882) devoted an entire book to the creature. In his 1881 publication, *The formation of vegetable mould, through the action of worms, with observations on their habit*, Darwin wrote:

> The plough is one of the most ancient and most valuable of man's inventions; but long before he existed the land was in fact regularly ploughed, and still continues to be thus ploughed by earth-worms. It may be doubted whether there are many other animals which have played so important a part in the history of the world, as have these lowly organised creatures.

More recently, Christopher Lloyd, author of *What on Earth Evolved? ... In Brief* (2009) also credited these 'subterranean wrigglers' as being the highest ranked of the 100 species that changed the world. Earthworms, it seems, deserve far more respect.

'A man may fish with the worm that hath eat of a king, and eat of the fish that hath fed of that worm.'

—William Shakespeare (1564–1616)

DAWN CHORUS

'Morning has broken, like the first morning
Blackbird has spoken, like the first bird'

The first Sunday of May is International Dawn Chorus
Day (ICDC). An event described by the Wildlife Trust
as 'the worldwide celebration of Nature's daily miracle'.
Dawn is accompanied by thousands of individual birds
advertising their whereabouts and protecting their ter-
ritories. Together this avian choir awakens the new day
with birdsong. The time of the chorus varies around the
world, from around 4 a.m. in northern temperate areas,
6 a.m. in the tropics, and as late as 8 a.m. in the southern
hemisphere. The ICDC urges people to 'meet up as dawn
is breaking and enjoy the music as the sun rises'.

BIRD SONG

'When a bird sings, it's telling you what it is
and where it is.
Learn bird calls and open a new window on your birding.'
—The Cornell Lab of Ornithology

'Cock-a-doodle-doo!' is the morning call of the cock-
erel. Hens cluck, turkeys gobble, ducks quack, doves
coo, crows caw, cuckoos cuckoo. These sounds are generally familiar to most, but identifying individual bird
songs is extremely difficult to master, especially when
the singer is out of sight. It requires practice, persistence

and the constant willingness to listen. In *Bill Oddie's How to Watch Wildlife* (2008), the British ornithologist advices readers to take their 'ears, plenty of patience and a Zen-like calmness as you spend half an hour trying to catch sight of a mystery bird'; and, more prosaically, 'Binoculars to confirm identification'.

For the complete amateur, it is helpful to first familiarise yourself with bird songs. The obvious place to start is the world's largest online collection from Cornell Macaulay Library: 150,000 nature audio recordings free to the public. This includes recordings of 75 per cent of the world's known bird species. The Royal Society for the Protection of Birds (RSPB), BirdLife Australia, and other international ornithological organisations also share area-specific samples.

European birdwatchers may find the following devices helpful. Firstly, some phonetic renderings of bird songs:

Barn owl: 'screeeeeee!'

Blue tit: 'tee-tee-tee, tit-tit-tit'

Chaffinch: 'cha-cha-cha, cha-cha-cha, cha-cha-cha'

Chiffchaff: 'chiff-chaff, chiff-chaff, chiff-chaff'

Great tit: 'tea-cher, tea-cher'

House sparrow: 'chiddik, chiddik'

Kestrel: 'kee kee kee'

Treecreeper: (high-pitched) 'tsee tsee'

Simple descriptions of the sounds can also be a good reference point, and there are various mnemonics that can be used to help remember the connections:

Blackbird: melodic laid-back flute sound ('beautiful blackbird')

Bullfinch: quiet, short, single peeping note ('peeping bullfinch')

Dunnock: even 'diddly-diddly' song ('diddly-diddly dunnock')

Green finch: machine-gun-like piping notes ('green beret finch')

Robin: thin, wistful fluting ('wistful robin')

Song thrush: similar to blackbird, higher-pitched and repetitive ('say it twice song thrush')

Starling: squeaks, clicks and whistles, mimics other sounds

Wren: long, powerful trill in the middle ('ringing wren')

And if the song you hear sounds like one of the following phrases, here's who it is:

Collared dove: 'I don't know. I don't know'

Reed bunting: 'one two … one two … one'

Wood pigeon: 'My toe IS bleeding. My toe IS bleeding'

Yellowhammer: 'A little bit of bread and no cheeeeeese'

In the southern hemisphere the species are quite different. BirdLife Australia's 'Birds in Backyards' programme listed their top 40 chart of distinctive song calls in urban areas. The chart itself is interesting, but the grouping of sounds is even more useful.

Sorrows
Common Koel (1)
Fan-tailed Cuckoo (25)
Pallid Cuckoo (26)
Brush Cuckoo (27)

Screechers
Channel-billed Cuckoo (2)
Yellow-tailed Black-Cockatoo (10)
Sulphur-crested Cockatoo (16)
Galah (18)
Rainbow Lorikeet (33)
Long-billed (38)

Hooters
Southern Boobook (3)
Tawny Frogmouth (4)
Barn Owl (22)
Australian Owlet-nightjar (23)
Powerful Owl (24)

Carollers
Grey Butcherbird (5)
Australian Magpie (11)
Pied Currawong (12)

Whistlers
Willie Wagtail (6)
Common Blackbird (28)

Common Myna (29)

Common Starling (30)

Australian King-Parrot (32)

Crimson Rosella (34)

Spotted Pardalote (35)

Figbird (40)

Cacklers

Masked Lapwing (7)

Little Wattlebird (8)

Laughing Kookaburra (13)

Criers

Australian Raven (9)

Clocks

Red Wattlebird (14)

Cooers

Spotted Turtle-Dove (15)

Peepers

Magpie-lark (17)

Noisy Miner (19)

Silvereye (37)

Waverers

Red-whiskered Bulbul (20)

Black-faced Cuckoo-shrike (21)

Olive-backed Oriole (31)

Trillers

Superb Fairy-wren (36

Squeakers

New Holland Honeyeater (39)

If phonetics, mnemonics, sorrows, screechers, hooters, carollers, whistlers, cacklers, criers, clocks, cooers, peepers, waverers, trillers and squeakers are hurting your ears and making your mind go all a-flutter, fear not. Another way of identifying bird song may soon be widely available.

Mark Berres, an ornithologist from the University of Wisconsin-Madison, has developed the Wisconsin Electronic Bird Identification Resource Database (WeBIRD). This mobile phone app can record a nearby bird call, submit that song, and retrieve a positive identification of the species. 'Fostering a connection with wildlife is one of the ways we're going to save it,' explains Berres, 'and WeBIRD puts that connection to birds in the palm of your hand.'

BLACKBIRD

The nightingale has a lyre of gold,
The lark's is a clarion call,
And the blackbird plays but a boxwood flute,
But I love him best of all.

For his song is all of the joy of life,
And we in the mad, spring weather,
We two have listened till he sang
Our hearts and lips together.

—William Henley (1849–1903)

SILENT SPRING

Rachel Carson (1907–1964) is often credited as being the founder of the modern environmental movement.

The release of her 1962 book *Silent Spring* exposed how DDT (dichlorodiphenyltrichloroethane) and other chemicals were essentially poisoning the natural world. The book single-handedly challenged agricultural scientists and the US government, raised public awareness about chemical misuse, led to global changes in pesticide policies and DDT bans.

Carson is not revered by everyone. She did and still does attract some very vocal opposition. 'If man were to follow the teachings of Miss Carson,' stated chemical industry spokesman Robert White-Stevens, 'we would return to the Dark Ages, and the insects and diseases and vermin would once again inherit the earth.'

Today the main charge against Carson is that her role in banning DDT has indirectly led to millions of malarial deaths. The Competitive Enterprise Institute, a free-market public policy group in Washington DC, has set up a website, RachelWasWrong.org, to address 'the dangers associated with anti-technology views'.

An early *Punch* review of *Silent Spring* read, 'Profoundly disturbing, her book may come to be regarded as being to 20th-century science what *The Origin of Species* was to that of the 19th.' Rachel Carson's book continues to divide opinion in the 21st century.

> The 'control of nature' is a phrase conceived in arrogance, born of the Neanderthal age of biology and philosophy, when it was supposed that nature exists for the convenience of man.
> —Rachel Carson, *Silent Spring* (1962)

POISON

The *Oxford English Dictionary* defines poison as 'a substance that is capable of causing the illness or death of a living organism when introduced or absorbed'. These substances come in the form of proteins and chemical compounds. Poison has long enjoyed a reputation as an agent of murder and suicide. History has been laced with famous victims.

Athens, 339BC. Greek philosopher Socrates was found guilty of heresy. His sentence was death by hemlock at his own hand. By the Middle Ages, poisoning had become quite the fashion. The French called arsenic *poudre de succession*, 'inheritance powder'. In Venice, members of the Council of Ten carried out murder by poison for a fee. Lucrezia Borgia (1480–1519), of the House of Borgia, also gained a reputation as a femme fatale who poisoned the wine of family enemies during banquets.

Deadly potions are also prevalent in the works of William Shakespeare (1564–1616): henbane (*Hyoscyamus niger*), aconite (*Aconitum*), and deadly nightshade (*Atropa belladonna*) all make appearances. 'No, no, the drink, the drink—O my dear Hamlet—The drink, the drink! I am poison'd' are the famous last words of Gertrude, Queen of Denmark. The most heart-wrenching of all tragedies, *Romeo and Juliet*, also sees the title character taken by the ingestion of a fatal liquid: 'O true apothecary! Thy drugs are quick. Thus with a kiss I die.'

Roman Emperor Claudius, Pope Clement VII, and Holy Roman Emperor Charles VI all fell victim to mushroom poisoning. The notorious Death Cap (*Amanita phalloides*) bears a striking resemblance to the edible Paddy Straw (*Volvariella volvacea*). Due to this mistaken identity, it still accounts for 90 per cent of all fungi fatalities today.

Poison became a weapon for warfare, mass murder and espionage from the 20th century. In the First World War the German Army and Allies used sulfur mustard, or mustard gas, on each other. Nazi Germany later turned to hydrogen cyanide in their gas chambers, with devastating effect. Members of the Third Reich favoured cyanide capsules to take their own lives. The demise of Bulgarian dissident Georgi Markov (1929–1978), days after being at the sharp end of an umbrella on Waterloo Bridge, revealed that ricin-filled pellets were the choice of the KGB. Twenty-eight years later, the poisoning and slow death of Alexander Litvinenko (1962–2006) suggested that the Russian secret services had by then turned to radioactive polonium-210.

All this talk of deception, murder and death is a bit scary, but fear not. These statistics from the US Centers for Disease Control and Prevention (CDC) put the present threat of poisoning into perspective. The CDC found that of the 41,592 poisoning deaths in the United States in 2009, 76 per cent were unintentional and 8 per cent undetermined. Furthermore, 91 per cent of unintentional deaths were caused by prescription painkillers, cocaine or heroin. Forensic toxicologist Alfred Swaine Taylor (1806–1880) summed up the situation perfectly: 'A poison in a small dose is a medicine, a medicine in a large dose is a poison.'

DEADLY DELICACY

The *Tetraodontidae* family of Pacific fish have a unique ability of filling their mouth with water and inflating themselves into a prickly ball when under attack. Pufferfish, balloonfish, blowfish, globefish, swellfish and fugu (river pig), as they are more commonly known, also contain a powerful toxin (tetrodotoxin) 1,200 times more poisonous than cyanide. Their toxic livers, gonads, intestines, eyes, skin and blood may well deter potential predators, but they have not stopped the deadly fish from becoming a Japanese delicacy.

The fish is so poisonous that all chefs who prepare it must have trained for at least two years, passed a written test and been issued a government-approved licence. The expertise required is such that only 35 per cent of all applicants become licensed. IntraFish Media have reported that 20,000 tons of fugu is consumed every year in Japan. With roughly 3,800 certified fugu restaurants nationwide 800 in Tokyo, there is no doubting the popularity of this extreme cuisine.

So what are the risks of fugu being your last meal? If you dine in a licensed eatery, highly unlikely. According to Japan's Ministry of Health, Labour and Welfare 803 people were poisoned between 1989 and 2006, and 52 died. In the past ten years there has only been one reported death from eating in a licensed restaurant.

Cleanliness and precision are central to safe preparation. As freezing and thawing prior to organ removal can lead toxins to migrate to the flesh, fugu is still alive when selected. Once on the carving block, the tail and

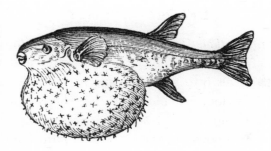

fins are chopped off, the mouth cut, skin peeled, eyes removed and flesh rinsed. The underside is sliced and great care taken not to burst the toxic innards during removal. All toxic parts are separated for later incineration. Edible flesh is cleaned, filleted and prepared. The 30-step process can take up to 20 minutes to complete.

Once prepared, fugu will be on the menu in various guises:

- Fugusashi: thin raw slices with ponzu sauce.
- Fugunabe or fuguchiri: blowfish slices and bones stewed with vegetables and konbu seaweed.
- Fugu no karaage: deep-fried slices rolled in potato starch, then salted.
- Shirako: blowfish testicles of the male blowfish.
- Hire-zake: fillet of grilled blowfish served in hot sake.

If any of these sound appetising and you enjoy the thrill of putting your life quite literally in the hands of a chef, this fish may well be for you.

Fugu poisoning symptoms:

1. If you get numbness in your mouth, try not to worry. This is part of the experience.

2. If this is followed by tingling in the extremities, headaches, nausea and paralysis of the face, you could be in trouble.

3. If respiratory distress, convulsions, speech impairment and cardiac arrhythmia strike, it has not been your lucky day. A zombie-like paralysis and death may follow.

VEGETABLE LAMB OF TARTARY

Medieval bestiaries presented mythical creatures alongside those found in the natural world. Dragons, unicorns, griffins and phoenix remain familiar today, through their presence in art, literature, heraldry, architecture and popular culture. But what happened to the Vegetable Lamb of Tartary, the fanciful plant-animal? With a past that brings together mystery, deception, and mistaken identity, it surely deserves a mention.

Also known as the Scythian Lamb and Barometz, this creature from Asia was first mentioned by Europeans in the 11th century. Lambs supposedly grew from seeds, remained attached to the plant supported by a stalk, and grazed in close proximity. Once pastures were out of reach, the animal would starve and the plant would die.

The somewhat fantastical *Travels of Sir John Mandeville* (c. 1357) added credibility of sorts, when he claimed the creature had been seen in India:

> There grew there a wonderful tree which bore tiny lambs on the endes of its branches. These branches were so pliable that they bent down to allow the lambs to feed when they are hungrie.

As the myth became more widely accepted, the golden fleeces of lambs supposedly grown from plants were imported, and sold for high prices. Explorers such as Engelbert Kaempfer (1651–1716) went in search of the curiosity, but to no avail. The evidence finally arrived in 1698 when Sir Hans Sloane presented a specimen to the Royal Society of London. The discovery of 'what is commonly, but falsely, in India, called "the Tartarian Lamb"' shattered centuries of myth-making. In the *Philosophical*

Transactions (1698) it was described in the following terms:

> more than a foot long, as big as one's wrist, having seven protuberances, and towards the end some foot-stalks about three or four inches long, exactly like the foot-stalks of ferns, both without and within. Most part of this was covered with a down of a dark yellowish snuff colour, some of it a quarter of an inch long.

The plant-animal was in fact the roots of a tree fern, with woolly stuff that resembled a fleece. This exhibit can still be seen today at the Museum of Garden History, London. The species itself was later named *Cibotium barometz* in honour of the legend.

The tale continued to fascinate naturalists. Erasmus Darwin (1731–1802) penned the following poem in his 1781 collection *The Botanic Garden*:

E'en round the Pole the flames of love aspire,
And icy bosoms feel the secret fire,
Cradled in snow, and fanned by Arctic air,
Shines, gentle borametz, thy golden hair
Rooted in earth, each cloven foot descends,
And round and round her flexile neck she bends,
Crops the grey coral moss, and hoary thyme,
Or laps with rosy tongue the melting rime;
Eyes with mute tenderness her distant dam,
And seems to bleat – a vegetable lamb.

The fiction had an added dimension after Henry Lee's 1887 book, *The Vegetable Lamb of Tartary; A Curious Fable of the Cotton Plant*. Lee insisted the tale was interwoven with much earlier descriptions of the cotton plant. Theophrastus (371–287BC) and Pliny the Elder (AD23–79) had both made mention of wool-bearing trees in their own writings. By the medieval period northern Europeans were still unaware of the origin of imported cotton. All similar materials came from animals. With this in mind, the rise and general acceptance of this curious creation does not seem quite so absurd.

OZ AND THEM

Australian wildlife is otherworldly, eclectic, unlikely, colourful and dangerous. The possibility of seeing kangaroos, koalas, possums, wallabies and wombats in the wild attracts visitors from across the world. But we value animals in relation to our past, their familiarity and our vested interests.

Antipodean residents can be slightly less enthused. As the most commonly seen and heard marsupial, Brushtail possums (*Trichosurus vulpecula*) are regarded by many as a noisy nuisance. *Cosmos* magazine described kangaroos as 'the deadliest animal menace to drivers on the nation's roads'. And since being introduced to Kangaroo Island 90 years ago, the iconic koala has gained pest status, which led to a sterilisation and relocation programme from 1997.

Wildlife is also valued in a different way by farmers when it poses a threat to production and livelihood. If we want wool, for example, sheep have to feed. If forage is not plentiful, food must be bought.

A 2010 planning guide for Tasmanian primary producers set out the grazing equivalents of wild animals and domestic stock, revealing that:

- 2 Forester kangaroos
- 3 Bennett's wallabies
- 5 pademelons
- 6 wombats
- 12 brushtail possums
- 18 rabbits

Are each equivalent to one sheep. It is easy to see how the presence of certain animals would quickly eat into the profits.

WOOLLY THINKING

Sheep are not renowned for their intelligence. They stand in fields together eating grass – always together. They never seem to be alone. When a shepherd wants his flock to move, it is the sheepdog who understands the whistles and calls, it is the sheepdog who barks the orders. The sheep passively do as they are told, moving in unison, all baaing, together.

If a stray flock found itself in a village and started grazing in gardens, taking over the village park, and baaing on the bowling green, you would imagine that moving them on and preventing any future annoyance would be simple. Round them up, construct fences and install cattle grids. This is exactly what the residents of Marsden, Yorkshire, did in 2004. Much to their surprise, the sheep started returning to the village.

It turned out that these free grazing sheep were far more clever than anyone had imagined. 'They lie down on their side, or sometimes their back, and just roll over and over the grids until they are clear,' explained Conservative councillor Dorothy Lindley. They also hurdled 5ft (1.5m) fences and squeezed through 8in (20cm) gaps. Residents were amazed by their intuition. A National Farmers' Union spokeswoman also admitted to having 'never seen anything like it'. The National Sheep Association hinted that the public had underestimated the intelligence of the species, claiming that they 'have more brainpower than people are willing to give them credit for'.

More recently, the reputation of sheep as

woolly-brained simpletons is being challenged by science. Michael Marshall, writing for *New Scientist* in February 2011, called sheep 'the brightest mind in the farmyard', noting that there is evidence that they can:

- Recognise each other's faces
- Remember significant others for at least two years
- Discriminate between breeds, preferring to look at their own
- Group plants by family
- Memorise the correct route through a maze

University of Cambridge scientists Laura Avanzo and Jennifer Morton also revealed their findings on the cognitive faculties of sheep. Their neurodegeneration research had used genetically modified sheep carrying the defective gene that causes Huntington's disease in humans. The animals had been put through a series of memory tests, 'driven more by curiosity than expectation'. Much to the scientists' surprise, the sheep had:

- Learned to recognise different patterns in colours
- Changed their behaviour according to the pattern they were looking at
- Altered their behaviour based on the various shapes placed in front of them

When sheep are not doing everything together, they do have a mind of their own which can make 'executive decisions'. Morton sums it up nicely: 'Sheep live in a flock, and in a flock they're rather silly. When you work with them as individuals, they behave very differently.' Marsden residents – the bar has been raised. It seems you may be stuck with the marauding, commando-rolling, intelligent sheep for some time.

HOLY COW

'My favorite animal is steak,' American writer Fran Lebowitz once quipped. The sardonic phrase was meant to be cutting and comical. But with nearly 300 million beef cattle killed annually, it seems that many meat-eaters around the world shared this carnivorous favouritism.

In India it is a totally different story. An estimated 300 million cattle freely wander the streets. They are pampered, protected by law, honoured at least once a year and venerated as sacred animals. The reason: as Mahatma Gandhi (1869–1948) wrote, 'The central fact of Hinduism is cow protection.' For Hindus, cows have the symbolic role of the mother and are linked with stories about Krishna, who appeared 5,000 years ago and became a cowherd.

The prohibition on beef-eating is an important part of Hindu identity. So much so that when Indian historian Dwijendra Narayan Jha published *Holy Cow: Beef in Indian Dietary Traditions* (2002), a book which revealed that Hindus and Buddhists ate beef in ancient times, it was labelled blasphemous and he received death threats.

BEEF

Some nations have an insatiable appetite for beef. The United States Department of Agriculture (USDA) reported that Uruguay topped the annual consumption table for pounds eaten per person in 2010:

Uruguay	136.9
Argentina	123.0
United States	85.5
Brazil	83.3
Paraguay	78.5
Australia	77.8
Canada	65.3
New Zealand	64.4
Kazakhstan	59.1
Hong Kong	52.4

THE COW-PUNCHER'S ELEGY

Ranching, branding, driving, lassoing, trading, killing and eating cattle have left a real legacy in certain countries, most notably the United States. Cowboys have been romanticised on the big screen. The existence of buckaroos, cowpokes, cowhands and cowpunchers in rugged American terrains are enjoyed by worldwide audiences. Beyond the gun-slinging stereotypes of Westerns, cowboys and cowgirls had a unique relationship with the natural world. Arthur Chapman's poem 'The Cow-Puncher's Elegy', is a refreshing insight:

> I've ridden nigh a thousand leagues upon two
>   bands of steel,
> And it takes a grizzled Westerner to know just how
>   I feel;
> The ranches dot the strongholds of the old-time
>   saddlemen,
> And the glory of the cattle days can ne'er come
>   back again.
> Oh, the creak of saddle leather—
> Oh, the sting of upland weather
> When the cowmen roamed the foothills and drove
>   in ten thousand steers;
> Through the years, back in the dreaming,
> I can see the camp-fires gleaming,
> And the lowing of the night-herd sounds, all
>   faintly, in my ears.
>
> There's a checkerboard of fences on the vast and
>   wind-swept range;
> And the haystacks and the windmills make the
>   landscape new and strange,
> And the plains are full of farmers, with their
>   harrows and their ploughs;

On the roadsides loiter kidlets, who are 'driving
   home the cows!'
Oh, the quickly faded glory
Of the cowboy's brief, brief story!
How the old range beckons vainly in the sunshine
   and the rain!
Oh, the reek of roundup battle
And the thund'ring hoofs of cattle—
But why dream a useless day-dream, that can only
   give one pain?

Where have gone those trails historic, where the
   herders sought the mart?
Where have they gone the saucy cow-towns,
   where the gunman played his part?
Where has gone the Cattle Kingdom, with its
   armed, heroic strife?
Each has vanished like a bubble that has lived its
   little life.
Oh, the spurs we set a-jingling,
And the blood that went a-tingling
When we rode forth in the morning, chaps-clad
   knights in cavalcade;
And the mem'ries that come trooping,
And the spirits, sad and drooping,
When the cowman looks about him at the havoc
   Time has made.

From Out Where the West Begins (1917)
By Arthur Chapman (1873–1935)

ANTLERS

The bony appendages that grow from the skulls of male deer (stag, buck, hart, bull) are prized trophies for big game hunters, especially when still attached to the disembodied head. For the deer, antlers are seen as a sign of strength and fertility to potential female partners, and a powerful weapon when fighting opponents. Yet antlers are not a permanent fixture; they are shed and regrown every year.

The process is as follows:

1. Stags begin to lose their antlers in autumn.

2. New ones grow, covered in a vascular skin membrane called velvet. This provides blood and supplies nutrients and oxygen, allowing the antlers to grow faster than any other mammal bone

3. Once fully grown, the velvet is removed by rubbing against trees, and the bone dies

4. Fully grown, bare antlers are displayed near the end of the summer

Each year the antlers become larger and heavier. The image overleaf shows the gradual transformation over a seven-year period.

Year 1: burrs form

Year 2: longer branch formed

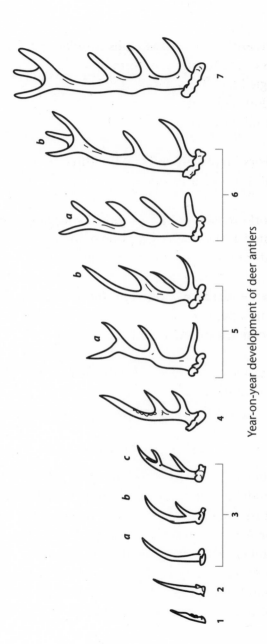

Year-on-year development of deer antlers

Year 3: the antler 'roses' – develops annular ridges around the bases of the horn. Takes form of:
a) a single branch
b) an additional fork
c) additional two forks

Year 4: Forks replace points. With three ends on each antler this is called a six-ender

Year 5: Forks replace points – a forked antler (as opposed to a pointed antler) has at least one branch on the upper two-thirds of the antler. These are eight-enders.

Year 6: Ten-ender in two different forms.
a) fork at upper end
b) crown at upper end

Year 7: Twelve-ender. Only crowns increase and change after the seventh year

SHED HUNTING

Shed antler hunting (or 'shed hunting') is a harmless way of adding a piece of nature into your home. The deer will be long gone and has no need for his former headwear. A word of warning: be careful where you hunt. In November 2011, an individual in southern Alberta was prosecuted and fined $345 for taking antlers from a Canadian National Park. A spokesperson for Waterton Lakes National Park told *Prairie Post West*: 'One reason we wanted to do this story is that in Alberta, you can do this [shed hunting], but not in our national parks. You can't take anything out. If you take it away others can't see it: it affects the visitor experience. And of course there's the wildlife: the [antlers] are quite a significant nutrient … I don't think I've ever found an antler that has not been chewed: they go back into the ecosystem in one way or another.' The individual was fortunate the judge showed leniency – the fine could have reached $25,000. That would have been an expensive reminder that you can look but not take away when visiting national parks.

HEALING THE MIND

In ancient Rome those struggling with low spirits would have been familiar with the phrase *Solvitur ambulando* – 'It is solved by walking'. Engaging with the natural world has long been appreciated as a way of making us feel better. According to American sociobiologist Edward O. Wilson, this happens because people have an innately emotional affinity with all other life forms. In his book *Biophilia* (1984), Wilson explains, 'The more we know of other forms of life, the more we enjoy and respect ourselves.' By placing nature over nurture, Wilson's concept has been met with scepticism and resistance. The idea of having an affiliation with nature has far fewer critics.

Richard Mabey, one of Britain's greatest nature writers, has felt totally disconnected from the natural world for periods of his life. The author makes no secret that a personal struggle with severe depression was the cause. In his 2005 memoir *Nature's Cure*, Mabey recounts an emotional journey charting his darkest moments and slow recovery. A rediscovery of nature proved to be the catalyst for the healing process: 'What healed me, I think, was ... a sense of being taken not out of myself but back in, of nature entering me, firing up the wild bits of my imagination.'

Closer to home, the power of pets should not be underestimated. They make us smile, they make us laugh, and they make us happy. The UK charity Pets as Therapy (PAT) has provided registered dogs and cats for therapeutic visits since 1983. The charity now has over 4,500 dogs and 108 cats on its books, which meet more than 130,000 people a week, offering 'companionship', 'happy associations', and 'unconditional love'. The counselling profession is also embracing the power of pets to work towards the psychological, physical and emotional goals of clients. HumAnima CIC involve a trained and temperament-assessed therapy dog in their sessions to help increase social interaction with peers through therapeutic activities.

Horses are also helping to address mental health and human development needs. The US-based organisation Equine Assisted Growth and Learning Association (EAGALA) trained 1,500 therapists in Britain in 2011. Meanwhile, UK charity Strength in Horses maintains that 'Interacting with such a powerful and spirited animal instils a sense of self-worth and self-confidence. This benefits in particular those people who as a result of prolonged mental distress and/or abuse have often experienced themselves as powerless.'

Independent animal encounter services, including Oreo and Friends and Critterish Allsorts, are now proving that pet therapy is not restricted to cats, dogs and horses. Skunks, raccoons, kinkajous, lizards, tortoises, snakes and spiders now frequent children's wards and mental health institutions across the UK, to be stroked, touched, played with or simply watched. For the patients this not only reduces blood pressure, it also releases naturally occurring feel-good hormones. In turn, stress and anxiety are reduced, and those involved become more mentally alert, increasingly relaxed and less sensitive to pain. With an increased heart rate, adrenalin output and a feeling of personal achievement, this emotion turns into excitement.

Asked for his views on reptile-assisted therapy, zoologist and TV personality Desmond Morris said, 'I think the shock of finding out how attractive these animals are, after all the bad press they have had, works wonders when they are encountered up close for the first time.'

HEALING HORSES

Winston Churchill (1874–1965) once famously observed, 'There's something about the outside of a horse that is good for the inside of a man.' Australian poet Pam Brown described the horse as a 'projection of peoples' dreams about themselves – strong, powerful, beautiful,' with 'the capability of giving us escape from our mundane existence.' In his 1997 autobiography *The Horses in My Life*, Monty Roberts' bond with horses seems to personify this capacity for emotional escapism:

> I had been riding horses before my memory kicked in, so my life with horses had no beginning. It simply appeared from the fog of infancy. I survived a difficult childhood by traveling on the backs of horses, and in adulthood the pattern didn't change.

Natural horsemanship entered the popular imagination with the release of Nicholas Evans's novel *The Horse Whisperer* in 1995, and the 1998 movie adaptation directed by and starring Robert Redford. The training technique in this story generally rejects violent methods, preferring a sympathetic approach which encourages empathy, cooperation and rapport between a practitioner and a horse.

The inspiration for the lead character in *The Horse Whisperer*, Tom Brooker, was American horse trainer Buck Brannaman. 'His skill, understanding and his gentle, loving heart have parted the clouds for countless troubled creatures. Buck is the Zen master of the horse world,' asserted author Evans. For Brannaman, 'Abused horses are like abused children. They trust no one and expect the worst. But patience, leadership, compassion and firmness can help them overcome their pasts.'

Horse whispering is not the only alternative practice used to overcome past experiences. Energy healing and animal communication is also recognised in the horse world. The leading expert, Dorset-based Margrit Coates, sets herself apart from Roberts and Brannaman, focusing on being and feeling rather than making and doing. Coates maintains, 'If we offer ourselves to our horses without agenda, being there for and with them, on their terms – we are rewarded and honoured with their wisdom, a huge and wonderful responsibility.' In *Healing for Horses* (2001) she explains that a human's touch should be 'as gentle as a butterfly' when treating a horse with hands-on healing.

Despite their differences, horse whispering and horse healing both prioritise the physical and mental well-being of individual animals. Remarkably, as the following quote from Xenophon (430–354BC) reveals, this way of thinking can be traced back to ancient Greece: 'For what the horse does under compulsion ... is done without understanding; and there is no beauty in it either, any more than if one should whip and spur a dancer.'

> 'With flowing tail and flying mane,
> Wide nostrils never stretched by pain,
> Mouth bloodless to bit or rein,
> And feet that iron never shod,
> And flanks unscarred by spur or rod,
> A thousand horse, the wild, the free,
> Like waves that follow o'er the sea,
> Came thickly thundering on.'
> —Lord Byron, *Mazeppa* (1818)

PET NATION

Seventy million European households own a pet. If, as Mahatma Gandhi (1869–1948) suggested, 'the greatness of a nation and its moral progress can be judged by the way its animals are treated', then Britain is truly Great. Almost half of all homes in the UK have animal companions, amounting to around 40 million fish, 7.4 million dogs, 7.3 million cats, 1 million indoor birds, 1 million rabbits, 400,000 hamsters, 300,000 frogs and toads ... the list goes on.

This is by no means a recent occurrence. Philip Howell explains 'the domestic dog was firmly installed at the heart of the respectable Victorian household, a kind of household god.' Pets became part of the family, emotional bonds were made, owners mourned when their companions died. Proof of this can be found in a secluded corner of Hyde Park, London, where over 300 pet tombstones stand.

The cemetery had a rather modest beginning, when the lodge keeper made the kind gesture of allowing a local family to bury their deceased Maltese Terrier. 'Poor Cherry. Died April 28. 1881,' reads the inscription. When other locals found out about this, they started bringing their former companions to the unofficial burial ground. Cherry was joined by Pupsey, Chin Chin, Scamp, Thomas, Minnie, Drag, Dolly, Freeky, Ba-Ba, Jim, Snap and many others. By 1903 the pet cemetery had become so popular it was full.

Pet cemeteries and crematoriums are now widely available in the UK. Animal companions can be remembered at dignified funerals and services. Ashes can be proudly displayed on the mantelpiece; bodies can be frozen or can become taxidermic subjects. And for those who are not so keen on urns or are unsettled by taxidermy, pet ashes can also be fired into sculptures resembling the animal companion.

> '39 per cent of London's pet owners purchased their pet for companionship, despite having 7.5 million neighbours across the city'.
>
> —Pet Food Manufacturers Association, 2008

DICKIN MEDAL

In 1943 Maria Dickin (1870–1951), founder of People's Dispensary for Sick Animals (PDSA) in 1917, introduced the highest award any animal can receive whilst serving in military conflict – the Dickin Medal. The bronze medal bears the words 'For Gallantry' and 'We Also Serve' within a laurel wreath; the striped green, brown and blue ribbon represents the naval, land and air forces. Internationally recognised as the animals' Victoria Cross, the specially commended medal has been awarded 64 times. Thirty-two pigeons, 28 dogs, three horses and one cat have been recognised for their gallantry and devotion to duty.

Take time to read the Roll of Honour citations for the first recipients of the respective species:

Pigeon

White Vision

Pigeon – SURP.41.L.3089

'For delivering a message under exceptionally difficult conditions and so contributing to the rescue of an Air Crew while serving with the RAF in October 1943.'

(Two other messenger pigeons, Winkie and Tyke, were awarded on the same day)

Awarded: 2 December 1943

Dog

Bob

Mongrel, 6th Royal West Kent Regt

'For constant devotion to duty with special mention of Patrol work at Green Hill, North Africa, while serving with the 6th Battalion Queens Own Royal West Kent Regt.'

Awarded: 24 March 1944

Horse

Olga

'On duty when a flying bomb demolished four houses in Tooting and a plate-glass window crashed immediately in front of her. Olga, after bolting for 100 yards, returned to the scene of the incident and remained on duty with her rider, controlling traffic and assisting rescue organisations.'

(Two other police horses, Upstart and Regal were awarded on the same day)

Awarded: 11 April 1947

Cat

Simon

'Served on HMS Amethyst during the Yangtze Incident, disposing of many rats though wounded by shell blast. Throughout the incident his behaviour was of the highest order, although the blast was capable of making a hole over a foot in diameter in a steel plate.'

Awarded: posthumously in 1949

The awarding of the medal was stopped in 1949 but revived in 2000 to posthumously honour Gander, a Newfoundland dog. The mascot of the Royal Rifles of Canada saved infantrymen during the Battle of Lye Mun, engaging the enemy and halting their advances. Gander was killed in action when gathering a grenade.

German shepherd Appollo next received the honour on 5 March 2002. New York Police Department dog Appollo represented all the Search and Rescue dogs at Ground Zero and the Pentagon following the terrorist attacks on 11 September 2001.

Labradors Salty and Roselle (guide dogs), Sam the German shepherd (Royal Army Veterinary Corps), Lucky the German shepherd (RAF Police anti-terrorist tracker), Sadie the Labrador (RAVC arms and explosive search), Treo the Labrador (RAVC, Arms and Explosives Search) and Theo the springer spaniel (RAVC, Arms and Explosives Search) have all since received the honour.

Other notable animal awards include the American Humane Association Hero Dog Awards™, created in 2010. Each year, eight 'ordinary dogs' which have done 'extraordinary things' gain national recognition for their bravery, loyalty and love. Categories include: enforcement and arson dog, service dog, therapy dog, military dog, guide dog, search and rescue dog, hearing dog and emerging hero dog.

In Britain, the British Animal Honours, founded in 2013, also celebrates the country's 'most extraordinary animals and the people who dedicate their lives to them'.

SKINNY PIGS

The name 'skinny pigs' conjures up images of malnourished farm animals, underfed swine, shall we say. It is in fact the pet name for a cavy or guinea pig that happens to be hairless. Apart from the minimal tufts of fur, usually on the nose and feet, their bodies are completely bald at birth.

Much like other 'hairless' animals, such as the Sphynx breed of cat, this particular strain of guinea pig divides opinion. But behind their unusual appearance is a sad past. They do not come from the wild – they have in fact descended from the laboratory. In 1978,

Montreal's Institute Armand Frappier (IAF) discovered a genetic mutation when four offspring from their cage-bred albino Hartley guinea pigs were born without hair. In 1982 this IAF hairless strain was sent to the Charles River Laboratories in Canada, where they were bred for animal research and used for dermatological testing.

Fortunately for these lab creations, in last ten years the confines of laboratories have been replaced by the comfort of people's homes in the United States, Canada, Scandinavia and more recently the UK. As pets, they must live in a warm, heated home as they would never survive the cold outside. On warm, sunny days they can graze in the garden, but need sun cream (factor 50+) so their delicate skin does not get burnt by the sun. They also have a higher metabolism than normal guinea pigs in order to maintain their body heat, which means they eat a lot of food.

On 20 February 2013 the *Daily Mail* reported:

> The RSPCA wouldn't recommend people buy these animals due to the welfare problems associated with selectively breeding them for lack of hair, and because they will have complex needs that must be met to keep them happy and healthy.

The skinny pig blurs ethical boundaries. A sub-species created by science, used for experimentation, but then valued as a pet. In terms of breeding, endangered species have a far more limited gene pool, yet society happily donates money for selective breeding programmes. If skinny pigs were not bred, they would become extinct outside of laboratories. Is this new strain of cavy not worth saving? The remaining lab animals, which are equally as sentient, continue being used for animal testing. Is their welfare not important?

With their delicate skin, skinny pigs are specialist pets, most suited to experienced, dare I say, responsible pet-owners. But as a species they are essentially guinea pigs without a coat, nothing more exotic. They do not care about their own appearance. As the product of experimentation, the skinny pig presents itself as the ideal animal to help raise awareness about unnecessary experimentation on animals for cosmetics testing – a practice which continues outside the EU.

In 1997 the UK banned the use of animals for testing cosmetic products. This was extended to include ingredients the following year. A full marketing ban on cosmetic products tested on animals elsewhere in the world came into place in the EU on 11 March 2013.

WILD AT HEART

July 1960, Tanzania. When 26-year-old primatologist Jane Goodall arrived at Gombe Stream Chimpanzee Reserve to study the Kasakela chimpanzee community, little was known about their behaviour in the wild. Within six months Goodall had observed human-like emotions, disproved the widely held belief they are primarily vegetarians, and witnessed co-operation and tool use.

At the same time, in the United States, captive chimpanzees were being trained by NASA and primed as donors in biomedical laboratories. As our closest animal relative, they seemed prime candidates for isolation, injections, incisions and other invasive procedures in the name of scientific progress. Their organs were also identified for use in cross-species transplantation.

Three surgeons attempted chimpanzee-to-human organ transplants in the 1960s: Keith Reemstma (kidneys), James Hardy (heart), and Thomas Starzl (liver). Needless to say, these transplants were neither successful nor popular. The longest-surviving recipient of kidneys lived for nine months, the heart patient died in two hours, and children who received livers lasted only days. All chimps, of course, were also killed. Such work was discontinued in America.

The first human-to-human heart transplant was performed by South African cardiac surgeon Christiaan Barnard (1922–2001) on 3 December 1967. A decade later, a lack of human donors, combined with advances in science, saw the surgeon briefly turn to chimpanzees. Barnard explained how he felt about this in his 1989 biography *Good Life Good Death*:

> I had ... two male chimps ... they lived next door to each other in separate cages ... before I used one as a donor. When we put him to sleep in his cage in preparation for the operation, he chattered and cried incessantly ... when we removed the body to the operating room, the other chimp wept bitterly

and was inconsolable for days. The incident made a deep impression on me. I vowed never again to experiment with such sensitive creatures.

For Bernard, emotion and ethics had prevailed.

The closeness of our primate cousins is being increasingly recognised. 'A zoologist from outer space would immediately classify us as just a third species of chimpanzee,' noted American scientist Jared Diamond in *The Rise and Fall of the Third Chimpanzee* (1992). The Chimpanzee Sequencing and Analysis Consortium have since compared the DNA sequences of chimps and humans. In 2005 they announced that the two genomes are almost 99 per cent identical, and after taking into account insertions and deletions still share 96 per cent of their sequence.

Alongside genetics, the cognitive similarity between humans and apes is also becoming legally accepted. Austria, Germany, Netherlands, New Zealand, Sweden and the United Kingdom have all introduced great ape research bans on those grounds. Only the United States and Gabon still use chimps for scientific research.

Dame Jane Goodall has gone on to dedicate her entire life to studying chimpanzees in the wild, establishing the Jane Goodall Institute, raising international awareness for the species and lobbying for their protection. 'It is time to rethink our mindless acceptance of animal experimentation in our labs,' Goodall argues. 'As long as chimpanzees are used in medical research, it is our responsibility to treat them as humanely as possible.'

PLANT PERCEPTION

Have you ever spoken to a plant? You know, a little word of encouragement when you are watering the pot plants, or a quiet compliment to the most beautiful flowers in your garden. Go on, be honest. You will be in good company. In 1986, Charles, Prince of Wales admitted, 'I just come and talk to the plants, really – very important to talk to them; they respond.'

This was by no means a new idea. Indian scientist Sir Jagadish Chandra Bose (1858–1937) had been doing 'astonishing experiments' on plants and flowers since 1900, hypothesising that they felt pain and understood affection. 'How are we to know what unseen changes take place within the plant?' Bose asked the audience at the Bengal Literary Conference in 1911. 'If it be excited or depressed by some special circumstance, how are we, on the outside, to be made aware of this?' Although the hypothesis was generally disregarded, Bose made a major contribution to the development of plant science, most notably biophysics.

Scientists continue in their attempts to prove plants have feelings. In 2002 German researchers found that plants release ethylene when attacked. Frank Kuhnemann, of Bonn University, explained, 'The more a plant is subjected to stress, the louder the signal we get on our microphone.'

So there is no need to be embarrassed – speak freely to your plants. When the potatoes are shaking in boiling water, and the onions are being chopped, it is alright to shed a tear. Plants have feelings too.

GIANTS OF THE FOREST

California is home to enormous trees blessed with longevity. Methuselah, a 4,700 year old Bristlecone Pine (*Pinus longaeva*), in the White Mountains of Inyo County, claims the record of the world's oldest continuously standing tree.

Today ancient specimens are protected, celebrated and admired, their existence and enormity sold as an experience. Tourists flock to the Avenue of the Giants, Humboldt Redwoods State Park, to be in the presence of the towering coastal redwoods (*Sequoia Sempervirens*) lining the highway. Each individual tree has its own story. At 950 years old and a height of 248 feet (75m) the 'Immortal Tree' is not the oldest or the tallest. It is dwarfed by fellow resident 'Hyperion' (379 feet/115m), the world's tallest living tree. What makes the Immortal Tree stand out is its ability to survive. Lightning strikes, logging attempts, forest fires and floods have not been able to take its life.

In the 19th century, immortality was wishful thinking. American-European expedition hunters first stumbled upon giant sequoia (*Sequoiadendron giganteum*) groves in 1833. The trees gained fame in 1852, when hunter Augustus T. Dowd (1823–1893) pursued an injured bear into unfamiliar territory. Dowd could not believe his eyes when he saw the giant redwoods, his story only being believed when others visited North Grove.

The largest specimen was the 'Discovery Tree' but a year after being named as such, this was chopped down and the bark reassembled to become a travelling exhibit.

The tree took five men 22 days to fell, and died 1,300 years young. The stump was subsequently used for dances.

Big trees meant big money for loggers. Their unimaginable size also made them star attractions at national exhibitions. People would pay good money to see the enormous trees. In 1854 businessman George Gale got his men to cut down the 'Mother of the Forest'; its reassembled bark was promoted as the largest tree in the world. The death of this giant, however, was not welcomed by all. The editors of *Gleason's Pictorial* wrote:

> To our mind, it seems a cruel idea, a perfect desecration, to cut down such a splendid tree ... what in the world could have possessed any mortal to embark in such a speculation with this mountain of wood?

With an estimated age of 2,520, such a desecration does appear particularly short-sighted. Yet this did not stop others making a quick profit from giant sequoias. A tree with a diameter of 24 feet (7.3m) was felled in 1875 and displayed at the Philadelphia Centennial Exhibition in 1876. Visitors refused to accept the outer shell had come from one tree and the exhibit became known as the 'California Hoax'.

No tree is immortal. They cannot live forever. What is certain is that the greed of humans significantly decreases their life expectancy.

PROMETHEUS

Profiteering is not the only factor to cut short the lives of ancient trees. Scientific curiosity has also led to premature deaths. In 1964 Donald Currey (1934–2004), a geography graduate, was studying the Little Ice Age in Wheeler Peak, eastern Nevada. When he attempted to age a Great Basin Bristlecone Pine (*Pinus longaeva*) known as 'Prometheus', his increment borer got stuck. Currey gained permission from the United States Forest Service to cut down 'specimen WPN-114' and it was sectioned and analysed. Much to the surprise of Currey, the Forest Service, scientists and the public, Prometheus was not only old; it was the oldest ever known unitary (non-clonal) organism. Its life ended at 5,000 years.

Radiocarbon dating completed in April 2008 found that the oldest known individual vegetatively cloned (where new individuals arise without seed or spore production) tree is a spruce found in Dalarna Province, Sweden. Although it is thought the trunk has lived for roughly 600 years, the root system has grown for 9,550 years. The man who discovered the tree, Leif Kullman, Professor of Physical Geography at Umeå University, nicknamed the tree 'Old Tjikko' after his late dog.

SAKURA SEASON

On 5 March 1598 Toyotomi Hideyoshi gathered 900 guests at the Daigoji Temple, Fushimi. The warrior who unified Japan did not want to talk about war; this was a cherry blossom (sakura) viewing party (Daigo-no-hanami). The flowering cherry tree has a special place in Japanese culture dating back to the Nara Period (710–794). In art and literature the blossom symbolises purity, simplicity, blood and the fleeting nature of life. The samurai valued this and Hideyoshi's event confirmed its role in the nation's broader cultural identity.

In modern Japan, sakura season continues to be celebrated. Every year the Japanese weather service and news media follow the cherry-blossom front advancing from Kyūshū in late March to Hokkaidō in the middle of May. Once in full bloom, the short-lived flowers usually float to the ground within a week. Crowds gather beneath the branches to savour the fleeting beauty while enjoying food, drink and general merriment.

THE FUTURE OF TREE DISEASES

August 1975. Reports of a deadly tree disease spreading across Britain could not match the pace of the infestation. More than 3 million trees had already perished due to Dutch elm disease. The Forestry Commission expected another 2 million elms to die that year. By 1979, the fungal infection carried by bark beetles had accounted for the death of over 30 million trees.

Edward Goldsmith (1928–2009), founder of *The*

Ecologist, lamented the dire situation in his article 'The Future of Tree Diseases':

> Elm, beech, sycamore, oak and ash make up the vast majority of the larger deciduous trees in this country. If the first of these is already being annihilated, and the second and third are afflicted – no one knows with what consequences – the prospect is indeed grim. If oak wilt were to cross the Atlantic, this would leave us with only the ash – a truly terrifying prospect.

The prospect has become even more terrifying than Goldsmith had imagined. In 2013, the one tree which appeared to be disease-free is now in the headlines, and at risk of being devastated by a new epidemic: ash dieback. Perhaps even more alarming is the fact that the majority of the public are oblivious to the other epidemics which continue to kill elm, beech, oak and other trees.

The Forestry Commission has announced there are nineteen pests and diseases attacking trees at present, ten of which are at an 'epidemic stage':

1. Alder phytophthora

First discovered in Britain in 1993, *Phytophthora alni* invades the stems and roots of alders, killing them. Up to a quarter of alders are already infected by the disease.

2. Ash dieback

Chalara fraxinea was first discovered at a Buckinghamshire nursery in February 2012. A consignment of infected trees had arrived from the Netherlands. By March 2013 there were 413 confirmed findings, nineteen in nursery sites, 221 in recently planted sites and 173 in established woodland. The *Chalara fraxinea* fungus causes leaf loss, crown dieback and tree death. It could wipe out a huge proportion of Britain's 92 million ash trees.

3. Bleeding canker
This is found in half the country's horse chestnut or conker trees. Rust-coloured bleeding legions eat into the bark, weakening the tree until it dies or has to be felled.

4. Chestnut leaf miner
This moth, *Cameraria ohridella*, first found in the London Borough of Wimbledon in July 2002, is now in most conker trees. Larvae mine within the leaves, weakening the tree. In combination with bleeding canker, this can lead to death.

5. Dutch elm disease
This arrived in two waves in the 1920s and 1960s, destroying most of the country's elm trees. Caused by two related species of fungi in the genus *Ophiostoma* and spread by various elm bark beetles, the disease continues to kill off mature trees.

6. *Phytophthora austrocedrae*
First discovered in the northern English Pennines in 2011. The pathogen has killed juniper in the Lake District and Scotland.

7. *Phytophthora lateralis*

This pathogen was first found in West Dunbartonshire, Scotland, in 2010. It has gone on to kill trees in western Scotland, Yorkshire, the South West and Wales. This root killing disease threatens to wipe out the popular ornamental Lawson cypress trees.

8. *Phytophthora pseudosyringae*

First recorded in Britain in 2005, this fungal disease causes root and collar rot in a number of trees. The beech tree is in danger of being wiped out.

9. Red band needle blight or dothistroma needle blight

The *Dothistroma septosporum* fungus was first found in Corsican pine in the 1950s. Defoliation weakens the host trees. This is a problem in conifer plantations, threatening native Scots pine across the UK.

10. *Phytophthora ramorum*

First found at a garden centre in Sussex in February 2002, the fungus-like pathogen is now widespread across south-west England, Wales and south-west Scotland. Japanese larch trees are widely affected. Attempts to prevent the spread of the disease have led to more than 4 million trees being felled.

For botanist and historical ecologist Oliver Rackham, the arrival of ash dieback and the other listed tree diseases is no surprise. In a November 2012 piece for the *Mail Online* he wrote:

What can I say about the new ash disease? I told you so. It fits a pattern that has been known, but not heeded, since my student days. I have been saying this for more than ten years in lectures and articles, and in my New Naturalist book *Woodlands*, published in 2006. The gravest threat to the world's trees and forests is not people cutting down trees, nor climate change, nor even too many deer: it is globalisation of tree diseases.

Rackham maintains that 'some of the responsibility lies with the tree-planting movement', which began with the government-sponsored Plant a Tree in '73 campaign. The institutionalisation and commercialisation of the craze has led to a focus on the quantity of trees, rather their quality, with cheap consignments being bought from infected areas across the world.

> 'It seems that any of the world's plant diseases is at liberty to enter Britain provided it does so via some other European Union country. By the time the problem has been detected and the bureaucracy has clanked into action, it is too late. Once a tree disease has become established in a country, it is almost unknown for it to be controlled, let alone exterminated.'
>
> —Oliver Rackham

CLONING

Cloning was once the staple of science fiction. Aldous Huxley's 1932 novel *Brave New World* presented a dystopian vision were human clones were industrially cultivated. Michael Crichton's *Jurassic Park* captivated readers and then movie-goers in the 1990s. The idea of cloning dinosaurs became established in popular culture, as did public curiosity of whether this could happen in reality. Scientists quelled the excitement, stressing its unlikelihood. Religious opponents condemned the human pursuit to 'play God'.

On 22 February 1997 the world became aware of the first mammal to be successfully cloned from an adult cell. Scientists from the Roslin Institute, Edinburgh, introduced the public to Dolly the sheep (1996–2003). Embryologist Dr Ian Wilmut announced that cloning would 'enable us to study genetic diseases for which there is presently no cure and track down the mechanisms that are involved.' Although Dolly was not the first clone – northern leopard frog tadpoles had been replicated in 1952 – this ewe became the face of cloning.

Genetically engineered cats, dogs, goats, sheep, pigs, cows and mice soon followed. The industrial cultivation of identical animals for the production of drugs, organs, meat and milk had become a reality. The resurrection of dinosaurs and human cloning must surely just be a matter of time. Evolutionary biologist Hendrik Poinar shared this view when interviewed by *National Geographic* in 2009: 'I laughed when Steven Spielberg said that cloning extinct animals was inevitable. But I'm not laughing anymore, at least about mammoths. This is going to happen. It's just a matter of working out the details.'

> 'God creates dinosaurs. God destroys dinosaurs.
> God creates man. Man destroys God.
> Man creates dinosaurs ...'
>
> Jeff Goldblum as Dr Ian Malcolm in *Jurassic Park*, 1993

EXTINCTION

Since 1500AD there have been 844 documented extinctions – a figure, the IUCN admits 'grossly underrepresents the number of extinctions that have taken place in historic times'. Alongside this, the IUCN Red List of endangered species suggests that one in three amphibians, one in four mammals, one in five invertebrates, and one in eight birds face extinction.

The *Smithsonian* magazine discussed the biased nature of such estimates on 3 September 2012, revealing the dire situation faced by so many species:

> Research tends to focus on the big, the cuddly and the beautiful. Plenty of research is done on polar bears and tigers, but how about dung beetles and fungi, mollusks and mites? ... The values shown on those already dismal maps should likely be three times higher than what's reported, and regardless of whether we know about it, creatures are blinking out all over the planet, all of the time.

When Richard Gray of the *Daily Telegraph* asked Sir David Attenborough in 2012 which ten species he would save from extinction on his personal ark, he responded:

> There are a lot of animals today that face the same fate as the dodo ... I could choose those that grab the headlines – the majestic tiger, the spectacular polar bear, the beautiful snow leopard or the magnificent mountain gorilla. They are all animals that I wouldn't want to lose. But there are many other extraordinary creatures out there not in the limelight.

Attenborough went on to choose ten species which represented 'the outstanding diversity of nature' he had experienced and encountered during his 60-year career. His list included:

1. Black lion tamarin (*Leontopithecus chrysopygus*)
   New World monkey endemic to São Paulo State, Brazil.

2. Sumatran rhino (*Dicerorhinus sumatrensis*)
   Found in Sumatra, Borneo, and the Malay Peninsula.

3. Solenodon (*Solenodon paradoxus*)
   These venomous mammals resemble large shrews and occur in the Dominican Republic and Haiti.

4. Olm salamander (*Proteus anguinus*)
   Blind amphibians endemic to the subterranean waters of caves in central and southeastern Europe

5. Marvellous spatuletail (*Loddigesia mirabilis*)
   Hummingbird native to Peruvian forests

6. Darwin's frog (*Rhinoderma darwinii*)
   Reside in forest streams of Argentina and Chile. Males rear tadpoles inside their mouths.

7. Sunda pangolin (*Manis javanica*)
   Toothless mammal covered by rows of scales. Found over much of mainland Southeast Asia.

8. Priam's birdwing (*Ornithoptera priamus*)
   Butterfly found in north-east Australia, Bismarck Archipelago, Maluku Islands, New Guinea and Solomon Islands,

9. Northern quoll (*Dasyurus hallucatus*)
   Small carnivorous marsupial from Northern Australia.

10. Venus's flower basket (*Euplectella aspergillum*)
    Hexactinellid sponge of the deep ocean.

So what does the future hold for endangered species, for conservation, for nature? At the IUCN assembly in 1968 environmentalist Baba Dioum made the point that 'In the end, we will conserve only what we love. We will love only what we understand. We will understand only what we are taught.' If this is the case, it is time to be receptive to new ideas, to be guided by personal curiosity, and approach the natural world with an open heart and open mind.

ACKNOWLEDGEMENTS

I am indebted to editorial director Duncan Heath for welcoming me to the Icon Books stable of authors. As the brains behind the Magpie concept, Simon Flynn gave me wings and The Nature Magpie persona. I am most grateful to you both for this opportunity. On editorial duty, the advice and guidance of Robert Sharman was invaluable. Thank you for reining in the silliness. I doff my many caps to you. Henry Lord, top-notch publicist, thank you kind sir. Also thanks to Andrew Furlow and Stacey Croft for your tireless work on the sales and marketing front.

I would like to thank Desmond Morris for his inspirational insights, and Mark O'Shea for kindly giving up his time to give me a much-needed lesson in venomous snakes. David Alderton, Peter Knight and Richard Waller all indirectly contributed by valuing my approach to the natural world. Your ongoing support is much appreciated.

Many of the entry ideas bubbled up during conversations with the lovely Annie McLaren. Two book dedications would be greedy Annie, so on request, 'Intestines of the Earth' and 'Monkeyana' are dedicated to you. Mark Levett, your philosophising has ignited the imagination. So, which does come first, the chicken or the egg?

The fascinating entry suggestions from Waterstones booksellers were most welcome. Sadly only a few could be added. Erika Ling, you wanted to know more about the badger cull: 'TB or not TB' is for you. Sarah Nuttall, I hope you enjoy 'Woolly Thinking'. Alex Kouliakioti, stand tall with the 'Giants of the Forest'. Social media interaction has been thought-provoking, and the support of friends old and new, has not gone unnoticed. Stephen Bond, Ed Collett, Cheryl Court, Mark Flear, Alan Kay, Ben Niland, Karen Parkhill, David Beech, Karen Brown, Mark Peden, Dale Preece-Kelly, Sallie Elizabeth Bent, I salute you!

Last, and by no means least, I am forever grateful to my parents, Janice and Tim, and brother Chris, for their kindness, patience and belief. Without you this book would not have been possible.

Picture acknowledgements

Thanks to Nick Halliday for his excellent illustrations that appear throughout the book. Thanks also to Kenshiroh for the 'No durians' image on page 44; to Walt Inkster, the *Devil's Artisan*, for the images on pages 77, 186 and 194; and to the Garden Museum for the 'Vegetable Lamb of Tartary' image on page 190. The tiger image on page 113 is from a woodcut by Thomas Bewick.

BIBLIOGRAPHY

Many sources were consulted in the writing of this book. I have aimed to provide a comprehensive list of them and apologise if any have been inadvertently omitted.

Books/articles

Adams, Douglas and Carwardine, Mark, *Last Chance to See*, Arrow, London, 2009

Adams, William M., *Against Extinction: The Story of Conservation*, Earthscan, London, 2004

Allen, Daniel, *The cultural and historical geographies of otter hunting in Britain, 1830–1939* (PhD thesis), University of Nottingham, 2006

Allen, Daniel, *Otter*, Reaktion Books, London, 2010

Allen, Daniel, 'Animal Blood Sports, British Isles' in Nauright, John and Parrish, Charles (ed.) *Sports Around the World: History, Culture, Practice*, ABC-CLIO, Santa Barbara, 2012, pp. 13–15

Allen, Daniel, 'Pet Therapy with Reptiles', *Practical Reptile Keeping*, October 2012, pp. 8–10

Allen, Daniel, 'Meeting the Skinny Pigs', *Small Furry Pets*, Issue 4, Autumn 2012, pp. 40–2

Allen, Daniel, 'Snakewatching and other reptilian observations with Dr Desmond Morris', *Practical Reptile Keeping*, April 2013, pp. 8–12

Allen, Daniel, 'Fishery owner claims that otters ate 22,000 carp! Sues Environment Agency', *Wildlife Extra*, January 2013

Anon., 'Mercury, Samos, Minuteman: Great Triple Play in U.S. Space Race', *LIFE*, 10 February 1961, pp. 16–24

Backshall, Steve, *Venom*, New Holland, London, 2007

Barringer, David, 'Raining on Evolution's Parade', *i-D Magazine*, March/April 2006

Beauman, Fran, *The Pineapple: King of Fruits*, Vintage, London, 2006

Beckford, Peter, *Thoughts on Hunting: In a Series of Letters to a Friend*, Sarum, Salisbury, 1781

Botts, Lee and Krushelnicki, Bruce, *The Great Lakes: An Environmental Atlas and Resource Book*, Environmental Canada, Toronto, 1987

Bright, Michael (ed.), *1001 natural wonders you must see before you die*, Cassell Illustrated, London, 2009

Burrell, Harry, *The Platypus*, Angus & Robertson Limited, Sydney, 1927

Bywater, Michael, *Lost Worlds*, Granta Books, London, 2005

Carson, Rachel, *Silent Spring*, Penguin, London, 2002

Carwardine, Mark, *Last Chance to See*, Collins, London, 2009

Carwardine, Mark, *The Natural History Museum Animal Records*, Natural History Museum, London, 2010

Carwardine, Mark, *Mark Carwardine's Ultimate Wildlife Experiences*, Wanderlust Publications Ltd, London, 2012

Chaboud, Rene, *How Weather Works: Understanding the Elements*, Thames and Hudson, London, 1996

Chaline, Eric, *Fifty Animals that Changed the Course of History*, David & Charles, Newton Abbot, 2011

Charlton, Lionel Evelyn Oswald, *This Cruelty Called Sport!*, League Against Cruel Sports, London, 1939

Coates, Margrit, *Healing for Horses: The Essential Guide to Using Hands-on Healing Energy With Horses*, Rider Books, London, 2001

Conniff, Richard, *The Species Seekers*, Norton, London, 2011

Cronin, William, *Uncommon Ground: Rethinking the Human Place in Nature*, W.W. Norton & Co., New York, 1997

Darwin, Charles, *On the Origin of Species*, Oxford University Press, Oxford, 2008

Darwin, Charles, *The Descent of Man, and Selection in Relation to Sex*, Penguin Classics, London, 2004

Dawkins, Richard, *The Selfish Gene*, Folio Society, London, 2011

Deutsch, Jonathan and Murakhver, Natalya (ed.) *They Eat That? A Cultural Encyclopedia of Weird and Exotic Food from around the World*, ABC-CLIO, Santa Barbara, 2012

Diamond, Jared, *The Rise and Fall of the Third Chimpanzee*, Radius, London, 1991

Dickens, Charles, 'The "Good" Hippopotamus', *Household News*, 12 October 1850, pp. 40–51

Douglas, Marjory S., *The Everglades: River of Grass*, Pineapple Press, Sarasota, 1997

Durrell, Gerald, *Menagerie Manor*, Penguin Books, London, 1975

Durrell, Gerald, *The Stationary Ark*, Collins, London, 1976

Ellis, Shaun, *The Man Who Lives with Wolves*, HarperCollins, London, 2010

Evans, Nicholas, *The Horse Whisperer*, Bantam, London, 1995

Fitzpatrick, Patrick J., *Hurricanes: A Reference Handbook*, ABC-CLIO, Santa Barbara, 2006

Flynn, Simon, *The Science Magpie*, Icon Books, London, 2012

Franklin, Benjamin, *The Private Correspondence of Benjamin Franklin*, Henry Colburn, London, 1817

Gould, Stephen Jay, *Wonderful Life: The Burgess Shale and the Nature of History*, W.W. Norton, New York, 1989

Griffin, Emma, *Blood Sport: Hunting in Britain since 1066*, Yale University Press, London, 2007

Gross, Charles G., 'Hippocampus Minor and Man's Place in Nature: A Case Study in the Social Construction of Neuroanatomy', *Hippocampus*, Vol. 3, No. 4, October 1993, pp. 403–416

Gross, Charles G., *Brain, Vision, Memory: Tales in the History of Neuroscience*, MIT Press, London, 1998

Grunwald, Michael, *The Swamp: The Everglades, Florida, and the Politics of Paradise*, Simon & Schuster, New York, 2006

Guinness World Records 2013, Guinness World Records Limited, London, 2012

Hamblyn, Richard, *The Invention of Clouds*, Picador, London, 2011

Hamilton, James, *Volcano,* Reaktion Books, London, 2012

Hansbury-Tenison, Robin, *The Oxford Book of Exploration*, Oxford University Press, Oxford, 1993

Heidorm, Keith and Whitelaw, Ian, *The Field Guide to Natural Wonders*, A&C Black, London, 2010

Herzog, Hal, *Some We Love, Some We Hate, Some We Eat*, Harper Perennial, London, 2011

Hinchliffe, Steve, Allen, John, Lavau, Stephanie, Bingham, Nick and Carte, Simon, 'Biosecurity and the topologies of infected life: from borderlines to borderlands', *Transactions of the Institute of British Geographers*, 2012

Hoare, Philip, *Leviathan, or, The Whale*, Harper Collins, London, 2008

Hoyle, Richard (ed.), *Our Hunting Fathers. Field sports in England after 1850*, Carnegie Publishing, Lancaster, 2007

Huxley, Aldous, *Brave New World*, Vintage Classic, London, 2007

Huxley, Robert (ed.), *The Great Naturalists*, Thames & Hudson, London, 2007

Jepson, Paul and Ladle, Richard, *Conservation*, Oneworld, Oxford, 2010

Jha, Dwijendra Narayan, *Holy Cow: Beef in Indian Dietary Traditions*, Verso, London, 2002

Johnson, Johnson P., *The Armchair Naturalist: How to be Good at Nature Without Really Trying*, Icon Books, London, 2007

Kean, Hilda, *Animal Rights*, Reaktion Books, London, 1998

Kemp, Christopher, *Floating Gold*, Chicago University Press, 2012

Kirk, Ruth, *Snow*, University of Washington Press, London, 1998

Krakauer, Jon, *Into the Wild*, Pan Books, London, 2007

Lavers, Chris, *Why Elephants Have Big Ears*, Phoenix, London, 2001

Laws, Bill, *Fifty Plants that Changed the Course of History*, David & Charles, Newton Abbot, 2010

Lloyd, Christopher, *What On Earth Happened? … In Brief: The Planet, Life & People from the Big Bang to Present Day*, Bloomsbury, London, 2009

Lloyd, Christopher, *What On Earth Evolved? … In Brief: 100 Species that Changed the World*, Bloomsbury, London, 2010

Mabey, Richard, *The Oxford Book of Nature Writing*, Oxford University Press, Oxford, 1997

Mabey, Richard, *Nature Cure*, Random House, London, 2005

McNamee, Gregory, *Aelian's On the Nature of Animals*, Trinity University Press, San Antonio, 2011

Miller, Jonathan and Van Loon, Borin, *Darwin for Beginners*, Icon Books, Cambridge, 1992

Morris, Desmond, *The Naked Ape*, Vintage, London, 1994

Morris, Desmond, *The Animal Contract*, Virgin Books, London, 1995

Morris, Desmond, *Watching: Encounters with Humans and Other Animals*, Max, London, 2006

Morris, Ramona and Morris, Desmond, *Men and Snakes*, Sphere Books Ltd, London, 1968

Murray, John A. (ed.), *The Quotable Nature Lover*, The Lyons Press, New York, 1999

Mullan, Bob and Marvin, Garry, *Zoo Culture*, University of Illinois Press, Chicago, 1999

Nash, Roderick, *Wilderness and the American Mind*, Yale University Press, London, 2001

Nicholls, Henry, *The Way of The Panda*, Profile, London, 2010

Oddie, Bill, Moss, Stephen and Pitcher, Fiona, *Bill Oddie's How to Watch Wildlife*, HarperCollins, London, 2008

O'Shea, Mark, *Venomous Snakes of the World*, New Holland, London, 2005

Peterson, Dale and Goodall, Jane, *Visions of Caliban*, The University of Georgia Press, London

Philo, Chris and Wilbert, Chris, *Animal Spaces, Beastly Places: New Geographies of Human–Animal Relations*, Routledge, London, 2000

Pliny the Elder, *Natural History*, Penguin Classics, London, 1991

Pretor-Pinney, Gavin, *The Cloudspotter's Guide*, Sceptre, London, 2006

Punch Library, *Mr Punch with Rod and Gun*, The Educational Book Company Ltd, London, No Date

Quick, Tom, *Interpretations of London's Hippopotami, 1850–1878* (MSc thesis), London Centre for the History of Science, Medicine and Technology, 2007

Rastogi, Rekha, *Let Us Identify the Useful Trees*, Children's Book Trust, New Delhi, 2008

Reisser, Julia, Proietti, Maíra, Kinas, Paul and Sazima, Ivan, 'Photographic identification of sea turtles: method description and validation, with an estimation of tag loss', *Endangered Species Research*, Vol. 5, 2008, pp. 73–82

Ritvo, Harriet, *The Animal Estate*, Harvard University Press, Cambridge, 1987

Roberts, Monty, *The Horses in My Life*, Headline, London, 2004

Robinson, Andrew, *Earthquake*, Reaktion Books, London, 2012

Sax, Boria, *Crow*, Reaktion Books, London, 2003

Shanor, Karen and Kanwal, Jagmeet, *Bats Sing, Mice Giggle: The Surprising Science of Animals' Inner Lives*, Icon Books, London, 2011

Stapleford, David, *An Affair with Red Squirrels*, The Lark Press, Dereham, 2003

Stark, Tony, *Knife to the Heart: The Story of Transplant Surgery*, Macmillan, London, 1996

Statham, Michael and Statham, Helen, *Wallaby Proof Fencing: A Planning Guide for Tasmanian Primary Producers*, Tasmanian Institute of Agricultural Research, Hobart, April 2010

Stein, Seth, *Disaster Deferred*, Columbia University Press, Chichester, 2011

Stevens, Austin J., *The Last Snake Man*, Noir, Hereford, 2007

Stewart, Amy, *Wicked Plants*, Timber Press, London, 2010

Stewart, George Rippey, *Storm*, Random House, New York, 1941

Stott, Rebecca, *Oyster*, Reaktion Books, London, 2004

Struthers, Jane, *Red Sky at Night: The Book of Lost Country Wisdom*, Ebury Press, Chatham, 2009

Thornes, John E., *John Constable's Skies: A Fusion of Art and Science*, University of Birmingham Press, Birmingham, 1999

Thoreau, Henry David, *Walden; or, Life in the Woods*, Dover Publications Inc., New York, 1995

Tudge, Colin, *The Secret Life of Trees*, Penguin, London, 2006

Walsh, John Henry, *British Rural Sports*, Routledge & Co., London, 1856

White, Gilbert, *The Natural History of Selborne*, Penguin, London, 1977

Wilson, Edward O., *Biophilia*, Harvard University Press, London, 1984

Wolch, Jennifer and Emel, Jody, *Animal Geographies: Place, Politics, and Identity in the Nature–Culture Borderlands*, Verso, London, 1998

Wu, David Y.H. and Cheung, Sidney C.H., *The Globalisation of Chinese Food*, Routledge, London, 2004

Websites and online articles

http://en.wikipedia.org/

http://blogs.smithsonianmag.com/smartnews/2012/09/extinction-rates-are-biased-and-much-worse-than-you-thought/#ixzz2OD5tN4Rp

http://www.telegraph.co.uk/news/9637972/Sir-David-Attenborough-picks-10-animals-he-would-take-on-his-ark.html

http://www.sharkbay.org/assets/images/id-green-vs-loggerhead-turt.gif

http://www.gutenberg.org/files/8717/8717-h/8717-h.htm

http://www.turtles.org/

http://www.mnn.com/earth-matters/animals/stories/turtle-found-that-pooped-plastic-for-a-month-0

http://naturalhistoryofselborne.com/

http://www.defra.gov.uk/animal-diseases/notifiable/

http://www.defra.gov.uk/animal-diseases/a-z/bovine-tb/

http://www.tcs.cam.ac.uk/story_type/site_trail_story/i-recognise-ewe-clever-sheep-raise-the-baa/

http://news.bbc.co.uk/1/hi/uk/3938591.stm

http://www.newscientist.com/article/dn20109-zoologger-the-sharpest-mind-in-the-farmyard.html

http://www.dailymail.co.uk/sciencetech/article-1356069/Sheep-intelligent-make-executive-decisions.html#ixzz2LwCp9A3Q

http://www.brasil.gov.br/cop10-english/overview/biodiversity-in-brazil/brazil-a-megadiverse-country/br_model1?set_language=en

http://www.guardian.co.uk/books/2002/jul/13/historybooks.highereducation

http://www.pdsa.org.uk/

http://www.canadiangeographic.ca/magazine/dec12/beaver.asp

http://www.bbc.co.uk/news/magazine-16219305

http://www.bbc.co.uk/news/world-us-canada-15503106

http://news.nationalpost.com/2011/10/28/polar-bear-should-replace-beaver-as-canadian-national-emblem-senator-nicole-eaton/

http://sandwalk.blogspot.co.uk/2011/10/beavers-vs-polar-bears.html

http://www.members.shaw.ca/kcic1/beaver.html

http://www.canadiangeographic.ca/magazine/dec12/beaver2.asp

http://www.hww.ca/en/species/mammals/beaver.html

http://www.truffle-uk.co.uk/

http://www.trufflehunter.co.uk/

http://www.twainquotes.com/Bats.html

http://www.bats.org.uk/

http://www.iucnredlist.org/

http://iucn.org/

http://www.nbcnews.com/id/22057756/

http://www.birds.cornell.edu/Page.aspx?pid=1478

http://www.rspb.org.uk/

http://birdlife.org.au/

http://www.nhm.ac.uk/nature-online/science-of-natural-history/biographies/linnaeus/

http://www.ec.gc.ca/eau-water/678C2760-86E3-412B-B450-8D4D48D3173B/G.Lakes-Profile.gif

http://www.zoology.ubc.ca/~etaylor/413www/commun_dist2.html

http://friendsofastonseyot.org.uk/

http://www.birdsinbackyards.net/birds/featured/Top-40-Bird-Songs

http://www.rspb.org.uk/community/wildlife/b/notesonnature/default.aspx?PostSortBy=MostViewed&PageIndex=1

http://www.allaboutbirds.org/page.aspx?pid=1059

http://edition.cnn.com/2000/NATURE/11/20/bird.song.enn/

http://www.ucmp.berkeley.edu/glossary/gloss5/biome/

http://www.worldbiomes.com/

http://www.dailymail.co.uk/news/article-2281597/Animal-charity-hits-
　　rise-number-skinny-pigs-warning-hard-look-suffer-breeding.html

http://www.rangewriter.org/outwherewestbegins.htm

http://www.sciencedaily.com/releases/2012/08/120813155523.htm

http://www.sciencedaily.com/releases/2012/04/120405224845.htm

http://science.time.com/2012/01/31/invaders-how-burmese-pythons-
　　are-devouring-the-everglades/

http://science.time.com/2012/01/31/invaders-how-burmese-pythons-
　　are-devouring-the-everglades/#ixzz2JwyO23AXDorcas

http://www.myfwc.com/news/news-releases/2013/february/18/
　　python-challenge/

http://content.yudu.com/Library/A1uowk/PrairiePostWestNovem/
　　resources/3.htm

http://www.wisdomportal.com/Magpie.html

http://www.discoverwildlife.com/british-wildlife/
　　debunking-myths-about-magpies

http://christianity.about.com/od/biblestorysummaries/p/
　　creationstory.htm

http://www.sfgate.com/news/article/The-Deadly-Delicacy-Allure-of-
　　bird-s-nest-soup-2720734.php#ixzz22xFM2xyA

http://www.jordanresearch.co.uk/pubs.html

http://www.bbc.co.uk/news/world-asia-pacific-12274825

http://www.bbc.co.uk/news/business-18193981

http://www.guardian.co.uk/uk/the-northerner/2012/mar/20/william-
　　wordsworth-daffodils-rydal-mount-national-trust

http://www.imb.uq.edu.au/index.html?page=48437&pid=48437
　　&ntemplate=235

http://www.animalcontrol.com.au/rabbit.htm

http://australianmuseum.net.au/Cane-Toad

https://secure.fera.defra.gov.uk/nonnativespecies/index.
　　cfm?pageid=163

http://www.bbc.co.uk/news/uk-14428585

https://secure.fera.defra.gov.uk/nonnativespecies/index.
　　cfm?sectionid=7

https://secure.fera.defra.gov.uk/nonnativespecies/ots/otsMap.cfm

http://www.mnn.com/earth-matters/animals/stories/invasive-exotic-
　　animals-costing-us-billions-of-dollars

http://news.bbc.co.uk/1/hi/sci/tech/8615398.stm

http://www.environment-agency.gov.uk/news/132163.aspx

http://www.dailymail.co.uk/news/article-2244475/Black-Ivory-coffee-
Thailand-using-beans-digested-elephants.html

http://elibrary.unm.edu/sora/Wilson/v086n04/p0461-p0462.pdf

http://www.int-birdstrike.org/Amsterdam_Papers/IBSC25%20WPSA3.pdf

http://www.australiangeographic.com.au/journal/why-chillies-are-
hot-the-science-behind-the-heat.htm

http://people.biology.ufl.edu/dlevey/pdfs/2006%20J%20Chem%20
Ecol%20Tewksbury.pdf

http://sevennaturalwonders.org/category/the-original/

http://nature.n7w.com/

http://scienceblogs.com/zooillogix/2008/01/29/the-schmidt-sting-
pain-index/

http://scienceblogs.com/zooillogix/2008/03/03/interview-with-
dr-justin-o-sch/

http://www.wilderdom.com/evolution/BiophiliaHypothesis.html

http://www.sharkfriends.com/sharks/PBarticle.html

http://www.currentresults.com/Environment-Facts/Plants-Animals/
number-species.php

http://www.iucnredlist.org/documents/summarystatistics/2010_1RL_
Stats_Table_1.pdf

http://edition.cnn.com/2006/TECH/science/05/26/chicken.egg/

http://www.dailymail.co.uk/sciencetech/article-1294341/Chicken-
really-DID-come-egg-say-scientists.html

http://www.metro.co.uk/news/835020-the-chicken-came-first-not-
the-egg-scientists-prove

http://edition.cnn.com/2010/WORLD/europe/07/14/england.
chicken.egg.riddle/index.html

http://www.cbsnews.com/2100-205_162-6676542.html

http://globetrooper.com/notes/science-venomous-snake-bites/

http://listverse.com/2011/03/30/top-10-most-venomous-snakes/

http://www.buzzle.com/articles/types-of-snake-venom.html

http://www.reptilegardens.com/reptiles/snakes/venomous/worlds-
deadliest-snakes.php

http://www.time.com/time/specials/packages/article/
0,28804,1967235_1967238_1967227,00.html

http://www.nhc.noaa.gov/aboutnames.shtml#atl

http://nation.time.com/2012/08/24/the-most-destructive-u-s-
   hurricanes-of-all-time/#ixzz2BwUo4YP5
http://www.conservation.org/where/priority_areas/hotspots/
   Documents/CI_Biodiversity-Hotspots_2011_Map.pdf
http://www.cepf.net/where_we_work/Pages/hotspot_facts.aspx
http://80.253.108.111/voyages/beagle2.jpg
http://www.archaeology.org/1001/topten/egypt.html
http://www.christs.cam.ac.uk/darwin200/pages/index.php?page_id=c8
http://www.zsl.org/about-us/library/artefact-of-the-month-june-
   2008,912,AR.html
http://carlzimmer.com/books/descentofman/excerpt.html
http://www.zsl.org/about-us/library/artefact-of-the-month-june-
   2008,912,AR.html
http://www.victorianlondon.org/entertainment/londonzoo.htm
http://eng.hrosi.org/?id=26
http://www.victorianlondon.org/entertainment/londonzoo.htm
http://www.tufts.edu/alumni/magazine/spring2002/jumbo.html
http://virtualvictorian.blogspot.co.uk/2010/06/
   story-of-jumbo-elephant.html
http://www.ephemerasociety.org/articles/jumbomania.html
http://phys.org/news/2012-01-china-free-pandas-wild.html#jCp
http://www.nytimes.com/2006/02/12/national/12panda.html?_r=0
http://www.guardian.co.uk/commentisfree/2011/dec/02/
   pandas-edinburgh-zoo
http://www.news.com.au/national-old/wang-wang-leaves-giant-
   panda-debt-for-adelaide-zoo/story-e6frfkvr-1225976525886
http://www.telegraph.co.uk/earth/wildlife/6216775/Chris-Packha
   m-Giant-pandas-should-be-allowed-to-die-out.html
http://phys.org/news/2012-01-china-free-pandas-wild.html#jCp
http://www.johnworldpeace.com/edproc.html
http://www.nelsonearthday.net/index.htm
http://www.canadianliving.com/life/green_living/5_ways_to_
   celebrate_earth_day.php
http://earthquake.usgs.gov/earthquakes/eqarchives/year/byyear.php
http://www.globalchange.umich.edu/globalchange1/current/lectures/
   evolving_earth/evolving_earth.html
http://kids.britannica.com/comptons/art-156012/The-six-major-
   types-of-volcanic-eruptions-differ-in-their

http://news.bbc.co.uk/1/hi/sci/tech/8621992.stm

http://www.rc.umd.edu/reference/wcircle/wood.pdf

http://in.news.yahoo.com/photos/aamsutra-culture-chameleon-slideshow/

http://www.ptes.org/

http://tigertime.info/

http://www.peta.org.uk/

http://www.humanesociety.org/

http://cloudappreciationsociety.org/collecting/

http://cloudappreciationsociety.org/manifesto/

http://www.geocaching.com/seek/cache_details.aspx?guid=68282e7c-2c1a-4775-b259-865d8fcdcfc9

http://www.its.caltech.edu/~atomic/snowcrystals/class/class.htm

http://www.ultimateungulate.com/

http://www.yalealumnimagazine.com/issues/2008_09/gorillas.html

http://friendsofdarwin.com/articles/owen/

http://aleph0.clarku.edu/huxley/comm/Punch/Monkey.html

http://www.library.otago.ac.nz/exhibitions/darwin/cabinet11.html

http://darwin-online.org.uk/EditorialIntroductions/Freeman_TheDescentofMan.html

http://darwin-online.org.uk/converted/Ancillary/1884_Hague_ReminiscenceofDarwin_A77.html

http://www.ucl.ac.uk/news/ucl-views/0809/orangutan

http://www.britannica.com/EBchecked/topic/151902/Charles-Darwin/225885/On-the-Origin-of-Species

http://www.nhm.ac.uk/nature-online/evolution/tree-of-life/darwin-tree/index.html

http://evopalaeo.blogspot.co.uk/2012/03/tree-thinking-1.html#!/2012/03/tree-thinking-1.html

http://www.guardian.co.uk/theguardian/2011/jan/30/chimp-took-america-into-space

http://history.nasa.gov/animals.html

http://www.releasechimps.org/

http://www.genome.gov/15515096

http://www.ouramazingplanet.com/1993-ocean-deep-mysteries-exploration.html

http://www.mnn.com/earth-matters/wilderness-resources/photos/7-people-who-gave-up-on-civilization-to-live-in-the-wild/related-photos

http://www.vanityfair.com/culture/features/2004/05/timothy-treadwell200405

http://www.yellowstone-bearman.com/Tim_Treadwell.html

http://www.cr.nps.gov/

http://www.pbs.org/nationalparks/history/

http://www.naturalhistorymag.com/picks-from-the-past/271452/america-s-national-parks

http://www.idcd.info/index.asp

http://www.guardian.co.uk/global/blog/2012/sep/27/rachel-carson-silent-spring-legacy

http://www.pbs.org/wgbh/pages/frontline/shows/nature/disrupt/sspring.html

http://rachelwaswrong.org/about-us/

http://www.shakespeareauthority.com/

http://www.cdc.gov/homeandrecreationalsafety/poisoning/poisoning-factsheet.htm

http://dsc.discovery.com/tv-shows/curiosity/topics/5-cloned-animals.htm

http://ngm.nationalgeographic.com/2009/05/cloned-species/mueller-text

http://www.dailytelegraph.com.au/news/breaking-news/dolly-the-sheep-cloning-biologist-dies/story-e6freuz9-1226494061001

http://www.sciencedaily.com/articles/d/dolly_the_sheep.htm

http://socresonline.org.uk/4/3/nerlich.html

http://news.bbc.co.uk/onthisday/hi/dates/stories/february/22/newsid_4245000/4245877.stm

http://www.dailymail.co.uk/sciencetech/article-1334201/Dolly-reborn-Four-clones-created-sheep-changed-science.html

http://www.pethealthcouncil.co.uk/

http://www.scas.org.uk/

http://www.pfma.org.uk/

http://www.fediaf.org/

http://londoninsight.wordpress.com/2010/10/06/pet-cemetery-hyde-park/

http://species.asu.edu/

http://www.dailymail.co.uk/news/article-112942/Plants-talk-say-scientists.html#ixzz2EwZppYG2

http://secretgardening.wordpress.com/tag/david-attenborough/

http://thesmartset.com/article/article11221101.aspx

http://www.dhakamirror.com/feature/a-brief-life-sketch-of-sir-jagadish-chandra-bose/

http://www.dailymail.co.uk/news/article-478558/So-Charles-right--talk-plants-scientists-discover.html

http://www.niagaramuseum.com/redwood_art_unique.htm

http://www.radford.edu/~wkovarik/envhist/mother.html

http://www.monumentaltrees.com/en/trees/giantsequoia/history/

http://www.environmentalgraffiti.com/plants/news-oldest-living-things-earth?image=6

http://spicebush.blogspot.co.uk/2010/01/old-trees.html

http://www.terrain.org/essays/14/cohen.htm

http://www.fas.usda.gov

http://www.economist.com/blogs/graphicdetail/2012/04/daily-chart-17

http://friendsofastonseyot.org.uk/

http://www.birdsinbackyards.net/birds/featured/Top-40-Bird-Songs

http://www.rspb.org.uk/community/wildlife/b/notesonnature/default.aspx?PostSortBy=MostViewed&PageIndex=1

http://www.allaboutbirds.org/page.aspx?pid=1059

http://www.rachelcarson.org/

http://edition.cnn.com/2000/NATURE/11/20/bird.song.enn/

http://www.wildlifetrusts.org/sites/default/files/Great%20places%20to%20see%20otters.pdf

http://www.bbc.co.uk/blogs/natureuk/2010/10/charlie-hamilton-james-on-how.shtml

http://factsanddetails.com/japan.php?itemid=649

http://www.guardian.co.uk/lifeandstyle/2009/jan/29/blowfish-how-to-cook-japan

http://www.life.umd.edu/grad/mlfsc/zctsim/pufferintro.html

http://www.fda.gov/Food/ResourcesForYou/FoodIndustry/ucm085458.htm

http://www.ehow.com/way_5267136_japanese-preparing-globefish-called-fugu.html

http://www.intrafish.com/incoming/article1360503.ece

http://www.australiangeographic.com.au/journal/animals-getting-high-wildlife-getting-their-fix.htm

http://www.guardian.co.uk/world/2009/jun/25/wallabies-high-
tasmania-poppy-fields

http://www.abc.net.au/news/2009-06-25/happy-hops-damage-poppy-
crops/1332044

http://www.cosmosmagazine.com/news/2948/kangaroos-are-menace-
aussie-drivers

http://www.ohranger.com/everglades/marjory-douglas

http://www.nps.gov/ever/parknews/presskit.htm

http://www.sciencedaily.com/releases/2012/08/120813155523.htm

http://www.sciencedaily.com/releases/2012/04/120405224845.htm

http://science.time.com/2012/01/31/invaders-how-burmese-pythons-
are-devouring-the-everglades/

http://science.time.com/2012/01/31/invaders-how-burmese-pythons-
are-devouring-the-everglades/#ixzz2JwyO23AXDorcas

http://www.myfwc.com/news/news-releases/2013/february/18/
python-challenge/

http://www.iucncsg.org/pages/Crocodiles%2C-Alligators-or-
Gharials%3F.html

http://www.huffingtonpost.com/2011/12/06/power-plant-crocodiles-
monitored_n_1131278.html

http://www.huffingtonpost.com/2012/08/09/american-crocodiles-
hatch_n_1760354.html

http://www.nytimes.com/2010/09/13/technology/13roadkill.
html?_r=0

http://youmeandbiodiversity.files.wordpress.com/2012/02/cat_
evolution_tree1.jpg

http://www.bbc.co.uk/nature/animals/wildbritain/field_guides/
animal_tracks.shtml

http://www.stuff.co.nz/technology/2946551/
Frisky-kakapo-romps-to-fame

http://www.guardian.co.uk/lifeandstyle/2010/may/15/bbc-wildlife-
otters

http://www.otter.org/

http://www.otterspecialistgroup.org/